MW01532945

There is No Such Thing as Hate Speech

There is No Such Thing as Hate Speech

Chad Felix Greene

Blinkquen

There is No Such Thing as Hate Speech

ISBN-13: 978-1545530740

ISBN–10: 1545530742

First Edition

Printing 2017

Printed in the United State of America

Image source: National Gallery of Art

This is a book of parody.

No relation in ideology or worldview (except for maybe two) is assumed of any artist or persons represented within the art.

Thank you to

Michael J. Knowles, author of the Amazon bestselling title: *Reasons to Vote for Democrats: A Comprehensive Guide,* April 11, 2017 [ISBN-10: 1501180126]

for his creativity, humor and *cough selling brilliance *cough that inspired this book.

Table of Contents

Preface

Introduction

There is no such thing as hate speech. There is no such thing as hate speech. There is no such thing as hate speech. There is no such thing as hate speech. There is no such thing as hate speech. There is no such thing as hate speech. There is no such thing as hate speech. There is no such thing as hate speech. There is no such thing as hate speech.

There is no such thing as hate speech. There is no such thing as hate speech. There is

no such thing as hate speech. There is no such thing as hate speech. There is no such thing as hate speech. There is no such thing as hate speech. There is no such thing as hate speech. There is no such thing as hate speech. There is no such thing as hate speech.

There is no such thing as hate speech. There is no such thing as hate speech. There is no such thing as hate speech. There is no such thing as hate speech. There is no such thing as hate speech. There is no such thing as hate speech. There is no such thing as hate speech. There is no such thing as hate speech. There is no such thing as hate speech. There is no such thing as hate speech. There is no such thing as hate speech.

There is no such thing as hate speech. There is no such thing as hate speech. There is no such thing as hate speech. There is no such thing as hate speech. There is no such thing as hate speech. There is no such thing as hate

There is no such thing as hate speech.
MC F

speech. There is no such thing as hate There is no such thing as hate speech. There is no such thing as hate speech. There is no such thing as hate speech

There is no such thing as hate speech. There is no such thing as hate speech.

There is no such thing as hate speech. There is no such thing as hate speech. There is no such thing as hate speech. There is no such thing as hate speech. There is no such thing as hate speech. There is no such thing as hate speech. There is no such thing as hate speech. There is no such thing as hate speech.

There is no such thing as hate speech. There is no such thing as hate speech. There is no such thing as hate speech. There is no such thing as hate speech. There is no such thing as hate speech. There is no such thing as hate speech.

There is no such thing as hate speech.

There is no such thing as hate speech. There is no such thing as hate speech. There is no such thing as hate speech. There is no such thing as hate speech. There is no such thing as hate speech. There is no such thing as hate speech. There is no such thing as hate speech. There is no such thing as hate speech.

There is no such thing as hate speech. There is no such thing as hate speech. There is no such thing as hate speech. There is no such thing as hate speech. There is no such thing as hate speech. There is no such thing as hate speech. There is no such thing as hate speech. There is no such thing as hate speech. There is no such thing as hate speech. There is no such thing as hate speech. There is no such thing as hate speech.

There is no such thing as hate speech. There is no such thing as hate speech. There is no such thing as hate speech. There is no such thing as hate speech. There is no such thing as

hate speech. There is no such thing as hate speech. There is no such thing as hate speech. There is no such thing as hate speech. There is no such thing as hate speech. There is no such thing as hate speech. There is no such thing as hate speech. There is no such thing as hate speech. There is no such thing as hate speech. There is no such thing as hate speech. There is no such thing as hate speech. There is no such thing as hate speech. There is no such thing as hate speech. There is no such thing as hate speech. There is no such thing as hate speech.

There is no such thing as hate speech. There is no such thing as hate speech. There is no such thing as hate speech. There is no such thing as hate speech. There is no such thing as hate speech. There is no such thing as hate speech. There is no such thing as hate speech. There is no such thing as hate speech. There is

no such thing as hate speech. There is no such thing as hate speech.

There is no such thing as hate speech. There is no such thing as hate speech. There is no such thing as hate speech. There is no such thing as hate speech. There is no such thing as hate speech. There is no such thing as hate speech. There is no such thing as hate speech. There is no such thing as hate speech. There is no such thing as hate speech. There is no such thing as hate speech. There is no such thing as hate speech. There is no such thing as hate speech. There is no such thing as hate speech. There is no such thing as hate speech. There is no such thing as hate speech. There is no such thing as hate speech. There is no such thing as hate speech. There is no such thing as hate speech. There is no such thing as hate speech. There is no such

thing as hate speech. There is no such thing as hate speech.

There is no such thing as hate speech. There is no such thing as hate speech. There is no such thing as hate speech. There is no such thing as hate speech. There is no such thing as hate speech. There is no such thing as hate speech. There is no such thing as hate speech. There is no such thing as hate speech. There is no such thing as hate speech. There is no such thing as hate speech. There is no such thing as hate speech. There is no such thing as hate speech. There is no such thing as hate speech. There is no such thing as hate speech. There is no such thing as hate speech.

There is no such thing as hate speech. There is no such thing as hate speech. There is no such thing as hate speech. There is no such thing as hate speech. There is no such thing as hate speech. There is no such thing as hate speech.

There is no such thing as hate speech. There is no such thing as hate speech. There is no such thing as hate speech. There is no such thing as hate speech. There is no such thing as hate speech. There is no such thing as hate speech.

There is no such thing as hate speech.

There is No Such Thing as Hate Speech

1

Freedom of Speech

There is no such thing as hate speech. There is no such thing as hate speech. There is no such thing as hate speech. There is no such thing as hate speech. There is no such thing as hate speech. There is no such thing as hate speech. There is no such thing as hate speech. There is no such thing as hate speech. There is no such thing as hate speech.

There is no such thing as hate speech. There is no such thing as hate speech. There is no such thing as hate speech. There is no such thing as hate speech. There is no such thing as hate speech. There is no such thing as hate

speech. There is no such thing as hate speech. There is no such thing as hate speech. There is no such thing as hate speech.

There is no such thing as hate speech. There is no such thing as hate speech. There is no such thing as hate speech. There is no such thing as hate speech. There is no such thing as hate speech. There is no such thing as hate speech. There is no such thing as hate speech. There is no such thing as hate speech. There is no such thing as hate speech. There is no such thing as hate speech.

There is no such thing as hate speech. There is no such thing as hate speech. There is no such thing as hate speech. There is no such thing as hate speech. There is no such thing as hate speech. There is no such thing as hate speech. There is no such thing as hate speech. There is no such thing as hate speech. There is no such

There is no such thing as hate speech.

thing as hate speech. There is no such thing as hate speech. There is no such thing as hate speech. There is no such thing as hate speech. There is no such thing as hate speech. There is no such thing as hate speech.

There is no such thing as hate speech. There is no such thing as hate speech. There is no such thing as hate speech. There is no such thing as hate speech. There is no such thing as hate speech. There is no such thing as hate speech. There is no such thing as hate speech. There is no such thing as hate speech. There is no such thing as hate speech. There is no such thing as hate speech. There is no such thing as hate speech. There is no such thing as hate speech. There is no such thing as hate speech. There is no such thing as hate speech.

There is no such thing as hate speech. There is no such thing as hate speech. There is no such thing as hate speech. There is no such

thing as hate speech. There is no such thing as hate speech. There is no such thing as hate speech. There is no such thing as hate speech. There is no such thing as hate speech. There is no such thing as hate speech. There is no such thing as hate speech. There is no such thing as hate speech.

There is no such thing as hate speech. There is no such thing as hate speech. There is no such thing as hate speech. There is no such thing as hate speech. There is no such thing as hate speech. There is no such thing as hate speech. There is no such thing as hate speech. There is no such thing as hate speech. There is no such thing as hate speech. There is no such thing as hate speech. There is no such thing as hate speech. There is no such thing as hate speech. There is no such thing as hate speech. There is no such thing as hate speech. There is no such thing as

hate speech. There is no such thing as hate speech. There is no such thing as hate speech. There is no such thing as hate speech.

There is no such thing as hate speech. There is no such thing as hate speech. There is no such thing as hate speech. There is no such thing as hate speech. There is no such thing as hate speech. There is no such thing as hate speech. There is no such thing as hate speech. There is no such thing as hate speech. There is no such thing as hate speech.

There is no such thing as hate speech. There is no such thing as hate speech. There is no such thing as hate speech. There is no such thing as hate speech. There is no such thing as hate speech. There is no such thing as hate speech. There is no such thing as hate speech. There is no such thing as hate speech. There is no such thing as hate speech. There is no such thing as

hate speech. There is no such thing as hate speech. There is no such thing as hate speech. There is no such thing as hate speech. There is no such thing as hate speech. There is no such thing as hate speech. There is no such thing as hate speech. There is no such thing as hate speech. There is no such thing as hate speech. There is no such thing as hate speech. There is no such thing as hate speech. There is no such thing as hate speech. There is no such thing as hate speech.

There is no such thing as hate speech. There is no such thing as hate speech. There is no such thing as hate speech. There is no such thing as hate speech. There is no such thing as hate speech. There is no such thing as hate speech. There is no such thing as hate speech. There is no such thing as hate speech. There is no such thing as hate speech. There is no such thing as hate speech. There is no such thing as hate speech. There is no such thing as hate speech. There is no such thing as hate speech. There is no such thing as hate

speech. There is no such thing as hate speech. There is no such thing as hate speech. There is no such thing as hate speech. There is no such thing as hate speech.

There is no such thing as hate speech. There is no such thing as hate speech. There is no such thing as hate speech. There is no such thing as hate speech. There is no such thing as hate speech. There is no such thing as hate speech. There is no such thing as hate speech. There is no such thing as hate speech. There is no such thing as hate speech. There is no such thing as hate speech. There is no such thing as hate speech. There is no such thing as hate speech.

There is no such thing as hate speech.

2

To Speak is to Live

There is no such thing as hate speech. There is no such thing as hate speech. There is no such thing as hate speech. There is no such thing as hate speech. There is no such thing as hate speech. There is no such thing as hate speech. There is no such thing as hate speech. There is no such thing as hate speech. There is no such thing as hate speech.

There is no such thing as hate speech.
There is no such thing as
hate speech. There
is no such thing as hate,

There is no such
thing as hate speech. There is no
such thing as hate speech. There is
no such thing as hate,
speech.

There is no such thing as hate,
speech. There is no such
thing as hate speech. There is no such, thing
as hate speech. There is
no such thing as hate speech. There
is no such thing
as hate speech. There is
no such thing,

as hate speech.

There is no such thing as hate speech. There is no such thing as hate speech. There is no such thing as hate speech. There is no such

There is no such
thing as hate
speech.

thing as hate speech. There is no such thing as hate speech. There is no such thing as hate speech. There is no such thing as hate speech. There is no such thing as hate speech.

There is no such thing as hate speech. There is no such thing as hate speech. There is no such thing as hate speech. There is no such thing as hate speech. There is no such thing as hate speech. There is no such thing as hate speech. There is no such thing as hate speech. There is no such thing as hate speech. There is no such thing as hate speech. There is no such thing as hate speech. There is no such thing as hate speech. There is no such thing as hate speech. There is no such thing as hate speech.

There is no such thing as hate speech. There is no such thing as hate speech. There is no such thing as hate speech. There is no such thing as hate speech. There is no such thing as

hate speech. There is no such thing as hate speech. There is no such thing as hate speech. There is no such thing as hate speech. There is no such thing as hate speech. There is no such thing as hate speech. There is no such thing as hate speech. There is no such thing as hate speech. There is no such thing as hate speech. There is no such thing as hate speech. There is no such thing as hate speech. There is no such thing as hate speech. There is no such thing as hate speech.

There is no such thing as hate speech. There is no such thing as hate speech. There is no such thing as hate speech. There is no such thing as hate speech. There is no such thing as hate speech. There is no such thing as hate speech. There is no such thing as hate speech.

There is no such thing as hate speech. There is no such thing as hate speech. There is no such thing as hate speech. There is no such thing as hate speech. There is no such thing as hate speech. There is no such thing as hate speech.

There is no such thing as hate speech. There is no such thing as hate speech. There is no such thing as hate speech. There is no such thing as hate speech. There is no such thing as hate speech. There is no such thing as hate speech.

There is no such thing as hate speech. There is no such thing as hate speech. There is no such thing as hate speech. There is no such thing as hate speech. There is no such thing as hate speech. There is no such thing as hate speech. There is no such thing as hate speech. There is no such thing as hate speech. There is no such thing as hate speech. There is no such thing as hate speech. There is no such thing as hate

speech. There is no such thing as hate speech. There is no such thing as hate speech.

There is no such thing as hate speech. There is no such thing as hate speech. There is no such thing as hate speech. There is no such thing as hate speech. There is no such thing as hate speech. There is no such thing as hate speech. There is no such thing as hate speech. There is no such thing as hate speech. There is no such thing as hate speech. There is no such thing as hate speech. There is no such thing as hate speech. There is no such thing as hate speech.

There is no such thing as hate speech. There is no such thing as hate speech. There is no such thing as hate speech. There is no such thing as hate speech. There is no such thing as hate speech. There is no such thing as hate speech. There is no such thing as hate speech. There is no such thing as hate speech. There is no such thing as hate speech. There is no such

thing as hate speech. There is no such thing as hate speech. There is no such thing as hate speech. There is no such thing as hate speech. There is no such thing as hate speech. There is no such thing as hate speech. There is no such thing as hate speech. There is no such thing as hate speech. There is no such thing as hate speech. There is no such thing as hate speech. There is no such thing as hate speech.

There is
no such thing as hate speech.
There is no
such thing as hate speech. There
is no such thing as,
hate speech.
There is no such thing as
hate speech.

There is no such thing as hate speech. There is no such thing as hate speech. There is

no such thing as hate speech. There is no such thing as hate speech. There is no such thing as hate speech. There is no such thing as hate speech. There is no such thing as hate speech. There is no such thing as hate speech. There is no such thing as hate speech. There is no such thing as hate speech. There is no such thing as hate speech. There is no such thing as hate speech.

There is no such thing as hate speech. There is no such thing as hate speech. There is no such thing as hate speech. There is no such thing as hate speech. There is no such thing as hate speech. There is no such thing as hate speech. There is no such thing as hate speech. There is no such thing as hate speech. There is no such thing as hate speech. There is no such thing as hate speech. There is no such thing as hate speech. There is no such thing as hate speech. There is no such thing as hate speech.

3

The Heart of Speech

There is no such thing as hate speech. There is no such thing as hate speech. There is no such thing as hate speech. There is no such thing as hate speech. There is no such thing as hate speech. There is no such thing as hate speech. There is no such thing as hate speech. There is no such thing as hate speech. There is no such thing as hate speech.

There is no such thing as hate speech. There is no such thing as hate speech. There is no such thing as hate speech. There is no such thing as hate speech. There is no such thing as hate speech. There is no such thing as hate speech. There is no such thing as hate speech.

There is no such thing as hate speech. There is no such thing as hate speech.

There is no such thing as hate speech. There is no such thing as hate speech. There is no such thing as hate speech. There is no such thing as hate speech. There is no such thing as hate speech. There is no such thing as hate speech. There is no such thing as hate speech. There is no such thing as hate speech. There is no such thing as hate speech. There is no such thing as hate speech. There is no such thing as hate speech.

There is no such thing as hate speech. There is no such thing as hate speech. There is no such thing as hate speech. There is no such thing as hate speech. There is no such thing as hate speech. There is no such thing as hate speech. There is no such thing as hate speech. There is no such thing as hate speech. There is no such thing as hate speech.

There is no such thing as hate speech.

THERE IS NO SUCH THING AS HATE SPEECH

There is no such thing as hate speech. There is no such thing as hate speech. There is no such thing as hate speech.

There is no such thing as hate speech. There is no such thing as hate speech. There is no such thing as hate speech. There is no such thing as hate speech. There is no such thing as hate speech. There is no such thing as hate speech. There is no such thing as hate speech. There is no such thing as hate speech.

There is no such thing as hate speech. There is no such thing as hate speech. There is no such thing as hate speech. There is no such thing as hate speech. There is no such thing as hate speech. There is no such thing as hate speech. There is no such thing as hate speech. There is no such thing as hate speech. There is no such thing as hate speech. There is no such thing as hate speech. There is no such thing as hate speech. There is no such thing as hate speech.

There is no such thing as hate speech. There is no such thing as hate speech. There is no such thing as hate speech.

"There is no such thing as hate speech. There is no such thing as hate speech." There is, *"no such thing as hate speech."* There is no such thing as hate speech. *"There is no such thing as hate speech. There is no such thing as hate speech. There is no such thing as hate speech."* There is no such thing as hate speech. There is no such thing as hate speech. There is no such thing as hate speech. There is no such thing as hate speech.

"There is no such thing as hate speech. There is no such thing as hate speech." There is, no such thing as "hate speech."

"There is"

"No such thing as hate speech."

"There is no such thing", as hate speech.

"There…"

"Is no such thing!'

"As hate speech. There is no such thing?'

"As hate speech…"

There is no such thing as hate speech. There is no such thing as hate speech. There is no such thing as hate speech. There is no such thing as hate speech. There is no such thing as hate speech. There is no such thing as hate speech. There is no such thing as hate speech. There is no such thing as hate speech. There is no such thing as hate speech. There is no such thing as hate speech. There is no such thing as hate speech.

There is no such thing as hate speech. There is no such thing as hate speech. *"There is no such thing",* as hate speech. There is no such thing as hate speech. There is no such thing as hate speech. There is no such thing as hate speech. There is no such thing as hate speech. There is no such thing as hate speech. There is no such thing as hate speech. There is no such thing as hate speech. There is no such thing as

hate speech. There is no such thing as hate speech.

"There is no such thing", as hate speech. "There is no such, thing as hate?"

"Speech!"

"There is no such thing as hate speech. There is no such thing."

"As hate speech. There is no such thing as hate speech. There is no such thing as hate speech. There is,"

"…no such thing as hate speech. There is no such thing as hate speech. There…"

"Is no such thing as hate speech!"

There is no such thing as hate speech. There is no such thing as hate speech. There is no such thing as hate speech. There is no such thing as hate speech. There is no such thing as hate speech. There is no such thing as hate speech. There is no such thing as hate speech. There is no such thing as hate speech. There is no such thing as hate speech. There is no such

thing as hate speech. There is no such thing as hate speech. There is no such thing as hate speech. There is no such thing as hate speech. There is no such thing as hate speech.

There is no such thing as hate speech. There is no such thing as hate speech. There is no such thing as hate speech. There is no such thing as hate speech. There is no such thing as hate speech. There is no such thing as hate speech. There is no such thing as hate speech. *"There is no such thing as hate speech. There is no such thing as hate speech."* There is no such thing as hate speech. There is no such thing as hate speech. There is no such thing as hate speech. There is no such thing as hate speech. There is no such thing as hate speech. There is no such thing as hate speech. There is no such thing as hate speech.

There is no such thing as hate speech. There is no such thing as hate speech. There is no such thing as hate speech. There is no such

thing as hate speech. There is no such thing as hate speech. There is no such thing as hate speech. There is no such thing as hate speech. There is no such thing as hate speech. There is no such thing as hate speech. There is no such thing as hate speech. There is no such thing as hate speech. There is no such thing as hate speech.

4

How Words Shape the World

There is no such thing as hate speech. There is no such thing as hate speech. There is no such thing as hate speech.

There is no such thing as hate speech. There is no such thing as hate speech. There is no such thing as hate speech. There is no such thing as hate speech. There is no such thing as hate speech. There is no such thing as hate speech.

There is no such thing as hate speech. There is no such thing as hate speech. There is no such thing as hate speech. There is no such

thing as hate speech. There is no such thing as hate speech. There is no such thing as hate speech. There is no such thing as hate speech. There is no such thing as hate speech. There is no such thing as hate speech.

There is no such thing as hate speech. There is no such thing as hate speech. There is no such thing as hate speech. There is no such thing as hate speech. There is no such thing as hate speech. There is no such thing as hate speech. There is no such thing as hate speech. There is no such thing as hate speech. There is no such thing as hate speech. There is no such thing as hate speech.

There is no such thing as hate speech. There is no such thing as hate speech. There is no such thing as hate speech. There is no such thing as hate speech. There is no such thing as hate speech. There is no such thing as hate speech. There is no such thing as hate speech.

THERE IS NO
SUCH THING
AS HATE
SPEECH!

There is no such thing as hate speech. There is no such thing as hate speech. There is no such thing as hate speech.

There is no such thing as hate speech. There is no such thing as hate speech. There is no such thing as hate speech. There is no such thing as hate speech. There is no such thing as hate speech. There is no such thing as hate speech. There is no such thing as hate speech.

There is no such thing as hate speech. There is no such thing as hate speech. There is no such thing as hate speech. There is no such thing as hate speech. There is no such thing as hate speech. There is no such thing as hate speech. There is no such thing as hate speech. There is no such thing as hate speech. There is no such thing as hate speech. There is no such thing as hate speech. There is no such thing as hate speech. There is no such thing as hate speech.

There is no such thing as hate speech. There is no such thing as hate speech.

There is no such thing as hate speech. There is no such thing as hate speech. There is no such thing as hate speech. There is no such thing as hate speech. There is no such thing as hate speech. There is no such thing as hate speech. There is no such thing as hate speech. There is no such thing as hate speech. There is no such thing as hate speech. There is no such thing as hate speech. There is no such thing as hate speech.

There is no such thing as hate speech. There is no such thing as hate speech. There is no such thing as hate speech. There is no such thing as hate speech. There is no such thing as hate speech. There is no such thing as hate speech. There is no such thing as hate speech. There is no such thing as hate speech. There is no such thing as hate speech. There is no such thing as hate speech. There is no such thing as

hate speech. There is no such thing as hate speech. There is no such thing as hate speech. There is no such thing as hate speech. There is no such thing as hate speech. There is no such thing as hate speech. There is no such thing as hate speech. There is no such thing as hate speech. There is no such thing as hate speech. There is no such thing as hate speech.

There is no such thing as hate speech. There is no such thing as hate speech. There is no such thing as hate speech. There is no such thing as hate speech. There is no such thing as hate speech. There is no such thing as hate speech. There is no such thing as hate speech. There is no such thing as hate speech. There is no such thing as hate speech. There is no such thing as hate speech.

There is no such thing as hate speech. There is no such thing as hate speech. There is no such thing as hate speech. There is no such thing as hate speech. There is no such thing as

hate speech. There is no such thing as hate speech. There is no such thing as hate speech. There is no such thing as hate speech. There is no such thing as hate speech. There is no such thing as hate speech. There is no such thing as hate speech. There is no such thing as hate speech. There is no such thing as hate speech. There is no such thing as hate speech. There is no such thing as hate speech. There is no such thing as hate speech. There is no such thing as hate speech. There is no such thing as hate speech. There is no such thing as hate speech. There is no such thing as hate speech. There is no such thing as hate speech. There is no such thing as hate speech.

There is no such thing as hate speech. There is no such thing as hate speech. There is no such thing as hate speech. There is no such thing as hate speech. There is no such thing as hate speech. There is no such thing as hate

speech. There is no such thing as hate speech. There is no such thing as hate speech. There is no such thing as hate speech. There is no such thing as hate speech. There is no such thing as hate speech. There is no such thing as hate speech. There is no such thing as hate speech. There is no such thing as hate speech. There is no such thing as hate speech. There is no such thing as hate speech.

There is no such thing as hate speech. There is no such thing as hate speech. There is no such thing as hate speech. There is no such thing as hate speech. There is no such thing as hate speech. There is no such thing as hate speech. There is no such thing as hate speech. There is no such thing as hate speech. There is no such thing as hate speech. There is no such thing as hate speech. There is no such thing as hate speech. There is no such thing as hate speech.

5

The Sound of Speech

There is no such thing as hate speech. There is no such thing as hate speech. There is no such thing as hate speech.

There is no such thing as hate speech. There is no such thing as hate speech. There is no such thing as hate speech. There is no such thing as hate speech. There is no such thing as hate speech. There is no such thing as hate speech.

There is no such thing as hate speech. There is no such thing as hate speech. There is no such thing as hate speech. There is no such thing as hate speech. There is no such thing as hate speech. There is no such thing as hate

speech. There is no such thing as hate speech. There is no such thing as hate speech. There is no such thing as hate speech.

There is no such thing as hate speech. There is no such thing as hate speech. There is no such thing as hate speech. There is no such thing as hate speech. There is no such thing as hate speech. There is no such thing as hate speech. There is no such thing as hate speech. There is no such thing as hate speech. There is no such thing as hate speech. There is no such thing as hate speech.

There is no such thing as hate speech. There is no such thing as hate speech. There is no such thing as hate speech. There is no such thing as hate speech. There is no such thing as hate speech. There is no such thing as hate speech. There is no such thing as hate speech. There is no such thing as hate speech. There is no such

There is no such
thing as hate speech

thing as hate speech. There is no such thing as hate speech. There is no such thing as hate speech.

There is no such thing as hate speech. There is no such thing as hate speech. There is no such thing as hate speech. There is no such thing as hate speech. There is no such thing as hate speech. There is no such thing as hate speech. There is no such thing as hate speech. There is no such thing as hate speech.

There is no such thing as hate speech. There is no such thing as hate speech. There is no such thing as hate speech. There is no such thing as hate speech. There is no such thing as hate speech. There is no such thing as hate speech. There is no such thing as hate speech. There is no such thing as hate speech. There is no such thing as hate speech. There is no such thing as hate speech. There is no such thing as hate speech. There is no such thing as hate speech. There is no such thing as hate speech.

There is no such thing as hate speech. There is no such thing as hate speech.

There is no such thing as hate speech. There is no such thing as hate speech. There is no such thing as hate speech. There is no such thing as hate speech. There is no such thing as hate speech. There is no such thing as hate speech. There is no such thing as hate speech. There is no such thing as hate speech. There is no such thing as hate speech. There is no such thing as hate speech. There is no such thing as hate speech.

There is no such thing as hate speech. There is no such thing as hate speech. There is no such thing as hate speech. There is no such thing as hate speech. There is no such thing as hate speech. There is no such thing as hate speech. There is no such thing as hate speech. There is no such thing as hate speech. There is no such thing as hate speech. There is no such thing as hate speech. There is no such thing as

hate speech. There is no such thing as hate speech. There is no such thing as hate speech. There is no such thing as hate speech. There is no such thing as hate speech. There is no such thing as hate speech. There is no such thing as hate speech. There is no such thing as hate speech. There is no such thing as hate speech. There is no such thing as hate speech.

There is no such thing as hate speech. There is no such thing as hate speech. There is no such thing as hate speech. There is no such thing as hate speech. There is no such thing as hate speech. There is no such thing as hate speech. There is no such thing as hate speech. There is no such thing as hate speech. There is no such thing as hate speech. There is no such thing as hate speech.

There is no such thing as hate speech. There is no such thing as hate speech. There is no such thing as hate speech. There is no such thing as hate speech. There is no such thing as

hate speech. There is no such thing as hate speech. There is no such thing as hate speech. There is no such thing as hate speech. There is no such thing as hate speech. There is no such thing as hate speech. There is no such thing as hate speech. There is no such thing as hate speech. There is no such thing as hate speech. There is no such thing as hate speech. There is no such thing as hate speech. There is no such thing as hate speech. There is no such thing as hate speech. There is no such thing as hate speech. There is no such thing as hate speech. There is no such thing as hate speech. There is no such thing as hate speech. There is no such thing as hate speech. There is no such thing as hate speech.

There is no such thing as hate speech. There is no such thing as hate speech. There is no such thing as hate speech. There is no such thing as hate speech. There is no such thing as hate speech. There is no such thing as hate

speech. There is no such thing as hate speech. There is no such thing as hate speech. There is no such thing as hate speech. There is no such thing as hate speech. There is no such thing as hate speech. There is no such thing as hate speech. There is no such thing as hate speech. There is no such thing as hate speech. There is no such thing as hate speech. There is no such thing as hate speech.

There is no such thing as hate speech. There is no such thing as hate speech. There is no such thing as hate speech. There is no such thing as hate speech. There is no such thing as hate speech. There is no such thing as hate speech. There is no such thing as hate speech. There is no such thing as hate speech. There is no such thing as hate speech. There is no such thing as hate speech. There is no such thing as hate speech.

There is no such thing as hate speech.

6

My Sister Speaks

There is no such thing as hate speech. There is no such thing as hate speech. There is no such thing as hate speech. There is no such thing as hate speech. There is no such thing as hate speech. There is no such thing as hate speech.

There is no such thing as hate speech. There is no such thing as hate speech. There is no such thing as hate speech. There is no such thing as hate speech. There is no such thing as hate speech. There is no such thing as hate speech. There is no such thing as hate speech. There is no such thing as hate speech. There is no such thing as hate speech.

There is no such thing as hate speech. There is no such thing as hate speech. There is no such thing as hate speech. There is no such thing as hate speech. There is no such thing as hate speech. There is no such thing as hate speech. There is no such thing as hate speech. There is no such thing as hate speech. There is no such thing as hate speech. There is no such thing as hate speech. There is no such thing as hate speech.

There is no such thing as hate speech. There is no such thing as hate speech. There is no such thing as hate speech. There is no such thing as hate speech. There is no such thing as hate speech. There is no such thing as hate speech. There is no such thing as hate speech. There is no such thing as hate speech. There is no such thing as hate speech. There is no such thing as hate speech. There is no such thing as hate speech

There is no such thing as hate speech.

There is no
such thing
as hate
speech...

There is no such thing as hate speech. There is no such thing as hate speech. There is no such thing as hate speech. There is no such thing as hate speech. There is no such thing as hate speech. There is no such thing as hate speech. There is no such thing as hate speech. There is no such thing as hate speech.

There is no such thing as hate speech. There is no such thing as hate speech. There is no such thing as hate speech. There is no such thing as hate speech. There is no such thing as hate speech. There is no such thing as hate speech. There is no such thing as hate speech. There is no such thing as hate speech. There is no such thing as hate speech. There is no such thing as hate speech. There is no such thing as hate speech. There is no such thing as hate speech. There is no such thing as hate speech. There is no such

thing as hate speech. There is no such thing as hate speech.

There is no such thing as hate speech. There is no such thing as hate speech. There is no such thing as hate speech. There is no such thing as hate speech. There is no such thing as hate speech. There is no such thing as hate speech. There is no such thing as hate speech. There is no such thing as hate speech. There is no such thing as hate speech. There is no such thing as hate speech. There is no such thing as hate speech.

There is no such thing as hate speech. There is no such thing as hate speech. There is no such thing as hate speech. There is no such thing as hate speech. There is no such thing as hate speech. There is no such thing as hate speech. There is no such thing as hate speech. There is no such thing as hate speech. There is no such thing as hate speech. There is no such thing as hate speech. There is no such thing as

hate speech. There is no such thing as hate speech. There is no such thing as hate speech. There is no such thing as hate speech. There is no such thing as hate speech. There is no such thing as hate speech. There is no such thing as hate speech. There is no such thing as hate speech. There is no such thing as hate speech. There is no such thing as hate speech.

There is no such thing as hate speech. There is no such thing as hate speech. There is no such thing as hate speech. There is no such thing as hate speech. There is no such thing as hate speech. There is no such thing as hate speech. There is no such thing as hate speech. There is no such thing as hate speech. There is no such thing as hate speech. There is no such thing as hate speech.

There is no such thing as hate speech. There is no such thing as hate speech. There is no such thing as hate speech. There is no such thing as hate speech. There is no such thing as

hate speech. There is no such thing as hate speech. There is no such thing as hate speech. There is no such thing as hate speech. There is no such thing as hate speech. There is no such thing as hate speech. There is no such thing as hate speech. There is no such thing as hate speech. There is no such thing as hate speech. There is no such thing as hate speech. There is no such thing as hate speech. There is no such thing as hate speech. There is no such thing as hate speech. There is no such thing as hate speech. There is no such thing as hate speech. There is no such thing as hate speech. There is no such thing as hate speech. There is no such thing as hate speech.

There is no such thing as hate speech. There is no such thing as hate speech. There is no such thing as hate speech. There is no such thing as hate speech. There is no such thing as hate speech. There is no such thing as hate

speech. There is no such thing as hate speech. There is no such thing as hate speech. There is no such thing as hate speech. There is no such thing as hate speech. There is no such thing as hate speech. There is no such thing as hate speech. There is no such thing as hate speech. There is no such thing as hate speech. There is no such thing as hate speech. There is no such thing as hate speech.

There is no such thing as hate speech. There is no such thing as hate speech. There is no such thing as hate speech. There is no such thing as hate speech. There is no such thing as hate speech. There is no such thing as hate speech. There is no such thing as hate speech. There is no such thing as hate speech. There is no such thing as hate speech. There is no such thing as hate speech. There is no such thing as hate speech. There is no such thing as hate speech.

There is no such thing as hate speech.

7

When the Words Were Heard

There is no such thing as hate speech. There is no such thing as hate speech. There is no such thing as hate speech.

There is no such thing as hate speech. There is no such thing as hate speech. There is no such thing as hate speech. There is no such thing as hate speech. There is no such thing as hate speech. There is no such thing as hate speech.

There is no such thing as hate speech. There is no such thing as hate speech. There is

no such thing as hate speech. There is no such thing as hate speech. There is no such thing as hate speech. There is no such thing as hate speech. There is no such thing as hate speech. There is no such thing as hate speech. There is no such thing as hate speech.

There is no such thing as hate speech. There is no such thing as hate speech. There is no such thing as hate speech. There is no such thing as hate speech. There is no such thing as hate speech. There is no such thing as hate speech. There is no such thing as hate speech. There is no such thing as hate speech. There is no such thing as hate speech. There is no such thing as hate speech. There is no such thing as hate speech.

There is no such thing as hate speech. There is no such thing as hate speech. There is no such thing as hate speech. There is no such thing as hate speech. There is no such thing as hate speech.

…there is no
such thing as a
hate crime…

There is no such thing as hate speech. There is no such thing as hate speech. There is no such thing as hate speech.

> *"There is no such thing as hate speech. There is no such thing as hate speech. There is no such thing as hate speech. There is no such thing as hate speech. There is no such thing as hate speech. There is no such thing as hate speech. There is no such thing as hate speech. There is no such thing as hate speech."*

There is no such thing as hate speech. There is no such thing as hate speech. There is no such thing as hate speech. There is no such thing as hate speech. There is no such thing as hate speech. There is no such thing as hate speech. There is no such thing as hate speech. There is no such thing as hate speech. There is no such thing as hate speech. There is no such thing as hate speech. There is no such thing as

hate speech. There is no such thing as hate speech. There is no such thing as hate speech. There is no such thing as hate speech. There is no such thing as hate speech.

There is no such thing as hate speech. There is no such thing as hate speech. There is no such thing as hate speech. There is no such thing as hate speech.

> *"There is no such thing as hate speech. There is no such thing as hate speech. There is no such thing as hate speech. There is no such thing as hate speech. There is no such thing as hate speech.*
>
> *There is no such thing as hate speech. There is no such thing as hate speech."*

There is no such thing as hate speech. There is no such thing as hate speech. There is no such thing as hate speech. There is no such thing as hate speech. There is no such thing as

hate speech. There is no such thing as hate speech. There is no such thing as hate speech. There is no such thing as hate speech. There is no such thing as hate speech. There is no such thing as hate speech.

There is no such thing as hate speech. There is no such thing as hate speech. There is no such thing as hate speech. There is no such thing as hate speech. There is no such thing as hate speech. There is no such thing as hate speech. There is no such thing as hate speech. There is no such thing as hate speech. There is no such thing as hate speech. There is no such thing as hate speech.

There is no such thing as hate speech. There is no such thing as hate speech. There is no such thing as hate speech. There is no such thing as hate speech. There is no such thing as hate speech. There is no such thing as hate speech. There is no such thing as hate speech. There is no such thing as hate speech. There is

no such thing as hate speech. There is no such thing as hate speech.

There is no such thing as hate speech. There is no such thing as hate speech. There is no such thing as hate speech. There is no such thing as hate speech. There is no such thing as hate speech. There is no such thing as hate speech. There is no such thing as hate speech. There is no such thing as hate speech.

> *"There is no such thing as hate speech. There is no such thing as hate speech. There is no such thing as hate speech. There is no such thing as hate speech. There is no such thing as hate speech. There is no such thing as hate speech. There is no such thing as hate speech. There is no such thing as hate speech."*

There is no such thing as hate speech. There is no such thing as hate speech. There is

no such thing as hate speech. There is no such thing as hate speech. There is no such thing as hate speech. There is no such thing as hate speech. There is no such thing as hate speech.

There is no such thing as hate speech. There is no such thing as hate speech. There is no such thing as hate speech. There is no such thing as hate speech. There is no such thing as hate speech. There is no such thing as hate speech. There is no such thing as hate speech. There is no such thing as hate speech. There is no such thing as hate speech. There is no such thing as hate speech. There is no such thing as hate speech. There is no such thing as hate speech. There is no such thing as hate speech. There is no such thing as hate speech. There is no such thing as hate speech.

There is no such thing as hate speech. There is no such thing as hate speech. There is no such thing as hate speech. There is no such

thing as hate speech. There is no such thing as hate speech. There is no such thing as hate speech. There is no such thing as hate speech. There is no such thing as hate speech. There is no such thing as hate speech. There is no such thing as hate speech. There is no such thing as hate speech. There is no such thing as hate speech.

There is no such thing as hate speech.

8

Divine Speech

There is no such thing as hate speech. There is no such thing as hate speech. There is no such thing as hate speech. There is no such thing as hate speech. There is no such thing as hate speech. There is no such thing as hate speech. There is no such thing as hate speech. There is no such thing as hate speech. There is no such thing as hate speech.

There is no such thing as hate speech. There is no such thing as hate speech. There is no such thing as hate speech. There is no such thing as hate speech. There is no such thing as hate speech. There is no such thing as hate speech. There is no such thing as hate speech.

There is no such thing as hate speech. There is no such thing as hate speech.

There is no such thing as hate speech. There is no such thing as hate speech. There is no such thing as hate speech. There is no such thing as hate speech. There is no such thing as hate speech. There is no such thing as hate speech. There is no such thing as hate speech. There is no such thing as hate speech. There is no such thing as hate speech. There is no such thing as hate speech. There is no such thing as hate speech.

There is no such thing as hate speech. There is no such thing as hate speech. There is no such thing as hate speech. There is no such thing as hate speech. There is no such thing as hate speech. There is no such thing as hate speech. There is no such thing as hate speech. There is no such thing as hate speech. There is no such thing as hate speech. There is no such

There is no
such thing
as hate
speech.

thing as hate speech. There is no such thing as hate speech. There is no such thing as hate speech.

There is no such thing as hate speech. There is no such thing as hate speech. There is no such thing as hate speech. There is no such thing as hate speech. There is no such thing as hate speech. There is no such thing as hate speech. There is no such thing as hate speech. There is no such thing as hate speech.

There is no such thing as hate speech. There is no such thing as hate speech. There is no such thing as hate speech. There is no such thing as hate speech. There is no such thing as hate speech. There is no such thing as hate speech. There is no such thing as hate speech. There is no such thing as hate speech. There is no such thing as hate speech. There is no such thing as hate speech. There is no such thing as hate speech. There is no such thing as hate speech.

There is no such thing as hate speech. There is no such thing as hate speech.

There is no such thing as hate speech. There is no such thing as hate speech. There is no such thing as hate speech. There is no such thing as hate speech. There is no such thing as hate speech. There is no such thing as hate speech. There is no such thing as hate speech. There is no such thing as hate speech. There is no such thing as hate speech. There is no such thing as hate speech. There is no such thing as hate speech.

There is no such thing as hate speech. There is no such thing as hate speech. There is no such thing as hate speech. There is no such thing as hate speech. There is no such thing as hate speech. There is no such thing as hate speech. There is no such thing as hate speech. There is no such thing as hate speech. There is no such thing as hate speech. There is no such thing as hate speech. There is no such thing as

hate speech. There is no such thing as hate speech. There is no such thing as hate speech. There is no such thing as hate speech. There is no such thing as hate speech. There is no such thing as hate speech. There is no such thing as hate speech. There is no such thing as hate speech. There is no such thing as hate speech. There is no such thing as hate speech.

There is no such thing as hate speech. There is no such thing as hate speech. There is no such thing as hate speech. There is no such thing as hate speech. There is no such thing as hate speech. There is no such thing as hate speech. There is no such thing as hate speech. There is no such thing as hate speech. There is no such thing as hate speech. There is no such thing as hate speech.

There is no such thing as hate speech. There is no such thing as hate speech. There is no such thing as hate speech. There is no such thing as hate speech. There is no such thing as

hate speech. There is no such thing as hate speech. There is no such thing as hate speech. There is no such thing as hate speech. There is no such thing as hate speech. There is no such thing as hate speech. There is no such thing as hate speech. There is no such thing as hate speech. There is no such thing as hate speech. There is no such thing as hate speech. There is no such thing as hate speech. There is no such thing as hate speech. There is no such thing as hate speech. There is no such thing as hate speech. There is no such thing as hate speech. There is no such thing as hate speech. There is no such thing as hate speech. There is no such thing as hate speech. There is no such thing as hate speech.

There is no such thing as hate speech. There is no such thing as hate speech. There is no such thing as hate speech. There is no such thing as hate speech. There is no such thing as hate speech. There is no such thing as hate

speech. There is no such thing as hate speech. There is no such thing as hate speech. There is no such thing as hate speech. There is no such thing as hate speech. There is no such thing as hate speech. There is no such thing as hate speech. There is no such thing as hate speech. There is no such thing as hate speech. There is no such thing as hate speech. There is no such thing as hate speech.

There is no such thing as hate speech. There is no such thing as hate speech. There is no such thing as hate speech. There is no such thing as hate speech. There is no such thing as hate speech. There is no such thing as hate speech. There is no such thing as hate speech. There is no such thing as hate speech. There is no such thing as hate speech. There is no such thing as hate speech. There is no such thing as hate speech. There is no such thing as hate speech. There is no such thing as hate speech.

9

So Many Things to Say

There is no such thing as hate speech. There is no such thing as hate speech. There is no such thing as hate speech.

There is no such thing as hate speech. There is no such thing as hate speech. There is no such thing as hate speech. There is no such thing as hate speech. There is no such thing as hate speech. There is no such thing as hate speech.

There is no such thing as hate speech. There is no such thing as hate speech. There is no such thing as hate speech. There is no such thing as hate speech. There is no such thing as hate speech. There is no such thing as hate

speech. There is no such thing as hate speech. There is no such thing as hate speech. There is no such thing as hate speech.

There is no such thing as hate speech. There is no such thing as hate speech. There is no such thing as hate speech. There is no such thing as hate speech. There is no such thing as hate speech. There is no such thing as hate speech. There is no such thing as hate speech. There is no such thing as hate speech. There is no such thing as hate speech. There is no such thing as hate speech.

There is no such thing as hate speech. There is no such thing as hate speech. There is no such thing as hate speech. There is no such thing as hate speech. There is no such thing as hate speech. There is no such thing as hate speech. There is no such thing as hate speech. There is no such thing as hate speech. There is no such

There is no such thing
as hate speech

thing as hate speech. There is no such thing as hate speech. There is no such thing as hate speech.

There is no such thing as hate speech. There is no such thing as hate speech. There is no such thing as hate speech. There is no such thing as hate speech. There is no such thing as hate speech. There is no such thing as hate speech. There is no such thing as hate speech. There is no such thing as hate speech.

There is no such
thing as hate speech.
There is no such thing as
hate speech. There
is no such thing as hate,
speech.
There is no such
thing as hate speech. There is no
such thing as hate speech. There is
no such thing as hate speech.

There is no such thing as hate,
speech. There is no such
thing as hate speech. There is no such,
thing as hate speech.

There is
no such thing as hate speech. There
is no such thing
as hate speech. There is
no such thing,
as hate speech.

There is no such thing as hate speech. There is no such thing as hate speech. There is no such thing as hate speech. There is no such thing as hate speech. There is no such thing as hate speech. There is no such thing as hate speech. There is no such thing as hate speech. There is no such thing as hate speech. There is no such thing as hate speech. There is no such thing as

hate speech. There is no such thing as hate speech. There is no such thing as hate speech. There is no such thing as hate speech. There is no such thing as hate speech. There is no such thing as hate speech.

There is no such thing as hate speech. There is no such thing as hate speech. There is no such thing as hate speech. There is no such thing as hate speech. There is no such thing as hate speech. There is no such thing as hate speech. There is no such thing as hate speech. There is no such thing as hate speech. There is no such thing as hate speech. There is no such thing as hate speech. There is no such thing as hate speech.

There is no such thing as hate speech. There is no such thing as hate speech. There is no such thing as hate speech. There is no such thing as hate speech. There is no such thing as hate speech. There is no such thing as hate speech. There is no such thing as hate speech.

There is no such thing as hate speech. There is no such thing as hate speech. There is no such thing as hate speech. There is no such thing as hate speech. There is no such thing as hate speech. There is no such thing as hate speech. There is no such thing as hate speech. There is no such thing as hate speech. There is no such thing as hate speech. There is no such thing as hate speech. There is no such thing as hate speech. There is no such thing as hate speech. There is no such thing as hate speech.

There is no such thing as hate speech. There is no such thing as hate speech. There is no such thing as hate speech. There is no such thing as hate speech. There is no such thing as hate speech. There is no such thing as hate speech. There is no such thing as hate speech. There is no such thing as hate speech. There is no such thing as hate speech. There is no such thing as hate speech. There is no such thing as hate speech.

There is no such thing as hate speech.

There is no such thing as
hate speech. There
is no such thing as hate,
speech.
There is no such
thing as hate speech. There is no
such thing as hate speech. There is
no such thing as hate,
speech.

There is no such thing as hate,
speech. There is no such
thing as hate speech. There is no such, thing
as hate speech. There is
no such thing as hate speech. There
is no such thing
as hate speech. There is
no such thing,

as hate speech.

There is no such thing as hate speech. There is no such thing as hate speech. There is no such thing as hate speech. There is no such thing as hate speech. There is no such thing as hate speech. There is no such thing as hate speech. There is no such thing as hate speech. There is no such thing as hate speech. There is no such thing as hate speech. There is no such thing as hate speech. There is no such thing as hate speech. There is no such thing as hate speech. There is no such thing as hate speech. There is no such thing as hate speech.

There is no such thing as hate speech. There is no such thing as hate speech. There is no such thing as hate speech. There is no such thing as hate speech. There is no such thing as hate speech. There is no such thing as hate speech. There is no such thing as hate speech. There is no such thing as hate speech. There is no such thing as hate speech. There is no such thing as hate speech.

There is no such thing as hate speech. There is no such thing as hate speech. There is no such thing as hate speech. There is no such thing as hate speech. There is no such thing as hate speech. There is no such thing as hate speech. There is no such thing as hate speech. There is no such thing as hate speech. There is no such thing as hate speech. There is no such thing as hate speech. There is no such thing as hate speech. There is no such thing as hate speech. There is no such thing as hate speech. There is no such thing as hate speech. There is no such thing as hate speech. There is no such thing as hate speech. There is no such thing as hate speech.

There is no such thing as hate speech. There is no such thing as hate speech. There is no such thing as hate speech. There is no such thing as hate speech. There is no such thing as hate speech. There is no such thing as hate speech. There is no such thing as hate speech. There is no such thing as hate speech. There is

no such thing as hate speech. There is no such thing as hate speech. There is no such thing as hate speech. There is no such thing as hate speech.

10

Introspection of Speech

There is no such thing as hate speech. There is no such thing as hate speech.

There is no such thing as hate speech. There is no such thing as hate speech. There is no such thing as hate speech. There is no such thing as hate speech. There is no such thing as hate speech. There is no such thing as hate speech.

There is no such thing as hate speech. There is no such thing as hate speech. There is no such thing as hate speech. There is no such thing as hate speech. There is no such thing as

hate speech. There is no such thing as hate speech. There is no such thing as hate speech. There is no such thing as hate speech. There is no such thing as hate speech.

There is no such thing as hate speech. There is no such thing as hate speech. There is no such thing as hate speech. There is no such thing as hate speech. There is no such thing as hate speech. There is no such thing as hate speech. There is no such thing as hate speech. There is no such thing as hate speech. There is no such thing as hate speech. There is no such thing as hate speech. There is no such thing as hate speech.

There is no such thing as hate speech. There is no such thing as hate speech. There is no such thing as hate speech. There is no such thing as hate speech. There is no such thing as hate speech. There is no such thing as hate speech. There is no such thing as hate speech.

There is no
such thing
as hate
speech.

There is no such thing as hate speech. There is no such thing as hate speech. There is no such thing as hate speech.

There is no such thing as hate speech. There is no such thing as hate speech. There is no such thing as hate speech. There is no such thing as hate speech. There is no such thing as hate speech. There is no such thing as hate speech. There is no such thing as hate speech. There is no such thing as hate speech.

There is no such thing as hate speech. There is no such thing as hate speech. There is no such thing as hate speech. There is no such thing as hate speech. There is no such thing as hate speech. There is no such thing as hate speech. There is no such thing as hate speech. There is no such thing as hate speech. There is no such thing as hate speech. There is no such thing as hate speech. There is no such thing as hate speech. There is no such thing as hate speech. There is no such thing as hate speech.

There is no such thing as hate speech. There is no such thing as hate speech.

"There is no such thing", as hate speech. "There is no such, thing as hate?"

"Speech!"

"There is no such thing as hate speech. There is no such thing."

"As hate speech. There is no such thing as hate speech. There is no such thing as hate speech. There is,"

"...no such thing as hate speech. There is no such thing as hate speech. There..."

"Is no such thing as hate speech!"

There is no such thing as hate speech. There is no such thing as hate speech. There is no such thing as hate speech. There is no such thing as hate speech. There is no such thing as hate speech. There is no such thing as hate speech. There is no such thing as hate speech. There is no such thing as hate speech. There is no such thing as hate speech. There is no such

thing as hate speech. There is no such thing as hate speech.

"There is no such thing", as hate speech. "There is no such, thing as hate speech!"

"There is no such thing as hate speech. There is no such thing. As hate speech. There is no such thing as hate speech. There is no such thing as hate speech. There is,"

"…no such thing as hate speech. There is no such thing as hate speech. There…"

"Is no such thing as hate speech!"

There is no such thing as hate speech. There is no such thing as hate speech. There is no such thing as hate speech. There is no such thing as hate speech. There is no such thing as hate speech. There is no such thing as hate speech. There is no such thing as hate speech. There is no such thing as hate speech. There is no such thing as hate speech. There is no such thing as hate speech. There is no such thing as hate speech. There is no such thing as hate

speech. There is no such thing as hate speech. There is no such thing as hate speech. There is no such thing as hate speech. There is no such thing as hate speech. There is no such thing as hate speech. There is no such thing as hate speech. There is no such thing as hate speech. There is no such thing as hate speech.

There is no such thing as hate speech. There is no such thing as hate speech. There is no such thing as hate speech. There is no such thing as hate speech. There is no such thing as hate speech. There is no such thing as hate speech. There is no such thing as hate speech. There is no such thing as hate speech. There is no such thing as hate speech. There is no such thing as hate speech.

There is no such thing as hate speech. There is no such thing as hate speech. There is no such thing as hate speech. There is no such thing as hate speech. There is no such thing as hate speech. There is no such thing as hate

speech. There is no such thing as hate speech. There is no such thing as hate speech. There is no such thing as hate speech. There is no such thing as hate speech. There is no such thing as hate speech. There is no such thing as hate speech. There is no such thing as hate speech. There is no such thing as hate speech. There is no such thing as hate speech. There is no such thing as hate speech. There is no such thing as hate speech. There is no such thing as hate speech. There is no such thing as hate speech. There is no such thing as hate speech. There is no such thing as hate speech. There is no such thing as hate speech.

There is no such thing as hate speech. There is no such thing as hate speech. There is no such thing as hate speech. There is no such thing as hate speech. There is no such thing as hate speech. There is no such thing as hate speech. There is no such thing as hate speech.

There is no such thing as hate speech. There is no such thing as hate speech. There is no such thing as hate speech. There is no such thing as hate speech. There is no such thing as hate speech. There is no such thing as hate speech. There is no such thing as hate speech. There is no such thing as hate speech. There is no such thing as hate speech.

> *"There is no such thing", as hate speech. There is no such, thing as hate speech!"*
>
> *"There is no such thing as hate speech. There is no such thing."*
>
> *"As hate speech. There is no such thing as hate speech. There is no such thing as hate speech. There is,"*
>
> *"…no such thing as hate speech. There is no such thing as hate speech. There…Is no such thing as hate speech!"*

There is no such thing as hate speech. There is no such thing as hate speech. There is no such thing as hate speech. There is no such

thing as hate speech. There is no such thing as hate speech. There is no such thing as hate speech. There is no such thing as hate speech. There is no such thing as hate speech. There is no such thing as hate speech. There is no such thing as hate speech. There is no such thing as hate speech. There is no such thing as hate speech.

11

If I Could Think in Words

There is no such thing as hate speech. There is no such thing as hate speech. There is no such thing as hate speech. There is no such thing as hate speech. There is no such thing as hate speech. There is no such thing as hate speech. There is no such thing as hate speech. There is no such thing as hate speech. There is no such thing as hate speech.

There is no such thing as hate speech. There is no such thing as hate speech. There is no such thing as hate speech. There is no such thing as hate speech. There is no such thing as

hate speech. There is no such thing as hate speech. There is no such thing as hate speech. There is no such thing as hate speech. There is no such thing as hate speech.

There is no such thing as hate speech. There is no such thing as hate speech. There is no such thing as hate speech. There is no such thing as hate speech. There is no such thing as hate speech. There is no such thing as hate speech. There is no such thing as hate speech. There is no such thing as hate speech. There is no such thing as hate speech. There is no such thing as hate speech. There is no such thing as hate speech.

There is no such thing as hate speech. There is no such thing as hate speech. There is no such thing as hate speech. There is no such thing as hate speech. There is no such thing as hate speech. There is no such thing as hate speech. There is no such thing as hate speech.

...there is no such thing as hate speech.

There is no such thing as hate speech. There is no such thing as hate speech. There is no such thing as hate speech.

There is no such thing as hate speech. There is no such thing as hate speech. There is no such thing as hate speech. There is no such thing as hate speech. There is no such thing as hate speech. There is no such thing as hate speech. There is no such thing as hate speech.

There is no such thing as hate speech. There is no such thing as hate speech. There is no such thing as hate speech. There is no such thing as hate speech. There is no such thing as hate speech. There is no such thing as hate speech. There is no such thing as hate speech. There is no such thing as hate speech. There is no such thing as hate speech. There is no such thing as hate speech. There is no such thing as hate speech.

There is no such thing as hate speech. There is no such thing as hate speech.

There is no such thing as hate speech. There is no such thing as hate speech. There is no such thing as hate speech. There is no such thing as hate speech. There is no such thing as hate speech. There is no such thing as hate speech. There is no such thing as hate speech. There is no such thing as hate speech. There is no such thing as hate speech. There is no such thing as hate speech. There is no such thing as hate speech.

There is no such thing as hate speech. There is no such thing as hate speech. There is no such thing as hate speech. There is no such thing as hate speech. There is no such thing as hate speech. There is no such thing as hate speech. There is no such thing as hate speech. There is no such thing as hate speech. There is no such thing as hate speech. There is no such thing as hate speech. There is no such thing as

hate speech. There is no such thing as hate speech. There is no such thing as hate speech. There is no such thing as hate speech. There is no such thing as hate speech. There is no such thing as hate speech. There is no such thing as hate speech. There is no such thing as hate speech. There is no such thing as hate speech. There is no such thing as hate speech.

There is no such thing as hate speech. There is no such thing as hate speech. There is no such thing as hate speech. There is no such thing as hate speech. There is no such thing as hate speech. There is no such thing as hate speech. There is no such thing as hate speech. There is no such thing as hate speech. There is no such thing as hate speech. There is no such thing as hate speech.

There is no such thing as hate speech. There is no such thing as hate speech. There is no such thing as hate speech. There is no such thing as hate speech. There is no such thing as

hate speech. There is no such thing as hate speech. There is no such thing as hate speech. There is no such thing as hate speech. There is no such thing as hate speech. There is no such thing as hate speech. There is no such thing as hate speech. There is no such thing as hate speech. There is no such thing as hate speech. There is no such thing as hate speech. There is no such thing as hate speech. There is no such thing as hate speech. There is no such thing as hate speech. There is no such thing as hate speech. There is no such thing as hate speech. There is no such thing as hate speech. There is no such thing as hate speech. There is no such thing as hate speech.

There is no such thing as hate speech. There is no such thing as hate speech. There is no such thing as hate speech. There is no such thing as hate speech. There is no such thing as hate speech. There is no such thing as hate

speech. There is no such thing as hate speech. There is no such thing as hate speech. There is no such thing as hate speech. There is no such thing as hate speech. There is no such thing as hate speech. There is no such thing as hate speech. There is no such thing as hate speech. There is no such thing as hate speech. There is no such thing as hate speech. There is no such thing as hate speech.

There is no such thing as hate speech. There is no such thing as hate speech. There is no such thing as hate speech. There is no such thing as hate speech. There is no such thing as hate speech. There is no such thing as hate speech. There is no such thing as hate speech. There is no such thing as hate speech. There is no such thing as hate speech. There is no such thing as hate speech. There is no such thing as hate speech. There is no such thing as hate speech.

12

The Innocence of Speech

There is no such thing as hate speech. There is no such thing as hate speech. There is no such thing as hate speech. There is no such thing as hate speech. There is no such thing as hate speech. There is no such thing as hate speech. There is no such thing as hate speech. There is no such thing as hate speech. There is no such thing as hate speech.

There is no such thing as hate speech. There is no such thing as hate speech. There is no such thing as hate speech. There is no such thing as hate speech. There is no such thing as

hate speech. There is no such thing as hate speech. There is no such thing as hate speech. There is no such thing as hate speech. There is no such thing as hate speech.

There is no such thing as hate speech. There is no such thing as hate speech. There is no such thing as hate speech. There is no such thing as hate speech. There is no such thing as hate speech. There is no such thing as hate speech. There is no such thing as hate speech. There is no such thing as hate speech. There is no such thing as hate speech. There is no such thing as hate speech. There is no such thing as hate speech.

There is no such thing as hate speech. There is no such thing as hate speech. There is no such thing as hate speech. There is no such thing as hate speech. There is no such thing as hate speech. There is no such thing as hate speech. There is no such thing as hate speech.

"There is no such thing as hate speech."

There is no
such thing as
hate speech!

There is no such thing as hate speech. There is no such thing as hate speech. There is no such thing as hate speech. There is no such thing as hate speech. There is no such thing as hate speech.

There is no such thing as hate speech. There is no such thing as hate speech. There is no such thing as hate speech. There is no such thing as hate speech. There is no such thing as hate speech. There is no such thing as hate speech. There is no such thing as hate speech. There is no such thing as hate speech.

There is no such thing as hate speech. There is no such thing as hate speech. There is no such thing as hate speech. There is no such thing as hate speech. There is no such thing as hate speech. There is no such thing as hate speech. There is no such thing as hate speech. There is no such thing as hate speech. There is no such

thing as hate speech. There is no such thing as hate speech. There is no such thing as hate speech. There is no such thing as hate speech. There is no such thing as hate speech. There is no such thing as hate speech.

There is no such thing as hate speech. There is no such thing as hate speech. There is no such thing as hate speech. There is no such thing as hate speech. There is no such thing as hate speech. There is no such thing as hate speech. There is no such thing as hate speech. There is no such thing as hate speech. There is no such thing as hate speech. There is no such thing as hate speech.

There is no such thing as hate speech. There is no such thing as hate speech. There is no such thing as hate speech. There is no such thing as hate speech. There is no such thing as hate speech. There is no such thing as hate speech. There is no such thing as hate speech.

There is no such thing as hate speech. There is no such thing as hate speech. There is no such thing as hate speech. There is no such thing as hate speech. There is no such thing as hate speech. There is no such thing as hate speech. There is no such thing as hate speech. There is no such thing as hate speech. There is no such thing as hate speech. There is no such thing as hate speech. There is no such thing as hate speech. There is no such thing as hate speech. There is no such thing as hate speech. There is no such thing as hate speech.

There is no such thing as hate speech. There is no such thing as hate speech. There is no such thing as hate speech. There is no such thing as hate speech. There is no such thing as hate speech. There is no such thing as hate speech. There is no such thing as hate speech. There is no such thing as hate speech. There is no such thing as hate speech. There is no such thing as hate speech. There is no such thing as hate speech.

There is no such thing as hate speech. There is no such thing as hate speech.

There is no such thing as hate speech. There is no such thing as hate speech. There is no such thing as hate speech. There is no such thing as hate speech. There is no such thing as hate speech. There is no such thing as hate speech. There is no such thing as hate speech. There is no such thing as hate speech. There is no such thing as hate speech. There is no such thing as hate speech. There is no such thing as hate speech. There is no such thing as hate speech. There is no such thing as hate speech. There is no such thing as hate speech. There is no such thing as hate speech. There is no such thing as hate speech.

There is no such thing as hate speech. There is no such thing as hate speech. There is no such thing as hate speech. There is no such thing as hate speech. There is no such thing as hate speech. There is no such thing as hate speech. There is no such thing as hate speech. There is no such thing as hate speech. There is

no such thing as hate speech. There is no such thing as hate speech. There is no such thing as hate speech. There is no such thing as hate speech. There is no such thing as hate speech. There is no such thing as hate speech. There is no such thing as hate speech. There is no such thing as hate speech. There is no such thing as hate speech.

There is no such thing as hate speech. There is no such thing as hate speech. There is no such thing as hate speech. There is no such thing as hate speech. There is no such thing as hate speech. There is no such thing as hate speech. There is no such thing as hate speech. There is no such thing as hate speech.

"There is no such thing as hate speech. There is no such thing…as hate speech."

There is no such thing as hate speech. There is no such thing as hate speech. There is no such thing as hate speech. There is no such thing as hate speech. There is no such thing as hate speech. There is no such thing as hate speech. There is no such thing as hate speech. There is no such thing as hate speech. There is no such thing as hate speech. There is no such thing as hate speech. There is no such thing as hate speech. There is no such thing as hate speech.

There is no such thing as hate speech. There is no such thing as hate speech. There is no such thing as hate speech. There is no such thing as hate speech. There is no such thing as hate speech. There is no such thing as hate speech. There is no such thing as hate speech. There is no such thing as hate speech. There is no such thing as hate speech. There is no such thing as hate speech. There is no such thing as hate

speech. There is no such thing as hate speech. There is no such thing as hate speech. There is no such thing as hate speech.

There is no such thing as hate speech. There is no such thing as hate speech. There is no such thing as hate speech. There is no such thing as hate speech. There is no such thing as hate speech. There is no such thing as hate speech. There is no such thing as hate speech. There is no such thing as hate speech. There is no such thing as hate speech. There is no such thing as hate speech. There is no such thing as hate speech. There is no such thing as hate speech. There is no such thing as hate speech. There is no such thing as hate speech. There is no such thing as hate speech.

There is no such thing as hate speech. There is no such thing as hate speech. There is no such thing as hate speech. There is no such thing as hate speech. There is no such thing as hate speech. There is no such thing as hate

speech. There is no such thing as hate speech. There is no such thing as hate speech. There is no such thing as hate speech. There is no such thing as hate speech. There is no such thing as hate speech. There is no such thing as hate speech. There is no such thing as hate speech. There is no such thing as hate speech. There is no such thing as hate speech.

There is no such thing as hate speech. There is no such thing as hate speech. There is no such thing as hate speech. There is no such thing as hate speech.

13

The Words are Suspect but True

There is no such thing as hate speech. There is no such thing as hate speech. There is no such thing as hate speech. There is no such thing as hate speech. There is no such thing as hate speech. There is no such thing as hate speech. There is no such thing as hate speech. There is no such thing as hate speech. There is no such thing as hate speech.

There is no such thing as hate speech. There is no such thing as hate speech. There is no such thing as hate speech. There is no such

thing as hate speech. There is no such thing as hate speech. There is no such thing as hate speech. There is no such thing as hate speech. There is no such thing as hate speech. There is no such thing as hate speech.

There is no such thing as hate speech. There is no such thing as hate speech. There is no such thing as hate speech. There is no such thing as hate speech. There is no such thing as hate speech. There is no such thing as hate speech. There is no such thing as hate speech. There is no such thing as hate speech. There is no such thing as hate speech. There is no such thing as hate speech. There is no such thing as hate speech.

There is no such thing as hate speech. There is no such thing as hate speech. There is no such thing as hate speech. There is no such thing as hate speech. There is no such thing as hate speech. There is no such thing as hate speech. There is no such thing as hate speech.

There is no
such thing as
hate speech.

There is no such thing as hate speech. There is no such thing as hate speech. There is no such thing as hate speech.

There is no such thing as hate speech. There is no such thing as hate speech. There is no such thing as hate speech. There is no such thing as hate speech. There is no such thing as hate speech. There is no such thing as hate speech. There is no such thing as hate speech. There is no such thing as hate speech.

"There is no such thing as hate speech. There is no such thing as hate speech. There is no such thing as hate speech. There is no such thing as hate speech. There is no such thing as hate speech. There is no such thing as hate speech. There is no such thing as hate speech."

There is no such thing as hate speech. There is no such thing as hate speech. There is no such thing as hate speech. There is no such

thing as hate speech. There is no such thing as hate speech. There is no such thing as hate speech. There is no such thing as hate speech. There is no such thing as hate speech.

"There is no such thing as hate speech. There is no such thing as hate speech. There is no such thing as hate speech."

There is no such thing as hate speech. There is no such thing as hate speech. There is no such thing as hate speech. There is no such thing as hate speech. There is no such thing as hate speech. There is no such thing as hate speech. There is no such thing as hate speech.

There is no such thing as hate speech. There is no such thing as hate speech. There is no such thing as hate speech. There is no such thing as hate speech. There is no such thing as hate

speech. There is no such thing as hate speech. There is no such thing as hate speech. There is no such thing as hate speech. There is no such thing as hate speech. There is no such thing as hate speech. There is no such thing as hate speech. There is no such thing as hate speech. There is no such thing as hate speech. There is no such thing as hate speech. There is no such thing as hate speech. There is no such thing as hate speech. There is no such thing as hate speech. There is no such thing as hate speech.

There is no such thing as hate speech. There is no such thing as hate speech. There is no such thing as hate speech. There is no such thing as hate speech. There is no such thing as hate speech. There is no such thing as hate speech. There is no such thing as hate speech. There is no such thing as hate speech. There is no such thing as hate speech. There is no such thing as hate speech.

There is no such thing as hate speech. There is no such thing as hate speech. There is no such thing as hate speech. There is no such thing as hate speech. There is no such thing as hate speech.

"There is no such thing as hate speech. There is no such thing as hate speech. There is no such thing as hate speech. There is no such thing as hate speech. There is no such thing as hate speech. There is no such thing as hate speech. There is no such thing as hate speech. There is no such thing as hate speech."

There is no such thing as hate speech. There is no such thing as hate speech. There is no such thing as hate speech. There is no such thing as hate speech. There is no such thing as hate speech. There is no such thing as hate speech. There is no such thing as hate speech. There is no such thing as hate speech. There is

no such thing as hate speech. There is no such thing as hate speech.

There is no such thing as hate speech. There is no such thing as hate speech. There is no such thing as hate speech. There is no such thing as hate speech. There is no such thing as hate speech. There is no such thing as hate speech. There is no such thing as hate speech. There is no such thing as hate speech. There is no such thing as hate speech. There is no such thing as hate speech. There is no such thing as hate speech. There is no such thing as hate speech. There is no such thing as hate speech. There is no such thing as hate speech. There is no such thing as hate speech.

There is no such thing as hate speech. There is no such thing as hate speech. There is no such thing as hate speech. There is no such thing as hate speech. There is no such thing as hate speech. There is no such thing as hate

speech. There is no such thing as hate speech. There is no such thing as hate speech. There is no such thing as hate speech. There is no such thing as hate speech. There is no such thing as hate speech. There is no such thing as hate speech.

14

When I Heard Words That Fought Back

There is no such thing as hate speech. There is no such thing as hate speech. There is no such thing as hate speech. There is no such thing as hate speech.

There is no such thing as hate speech. There is no such thing as hate speech. There is no such thing as hate speech. There is no such thing as hate speech. There is no such thing as hate speech.

There is no such thing as hate speech. There is no such thing as hate speech. There is

no such thing as hate speech. There is no such thing as hate speech. There is no such thing as hate speech. There is no such thing as hate speech. There is no such thing as hate speech. There is no such thing as hate speech. There is no such thing as hate speech.

There is no such thing as hate speech. There is no such thing as hate speech. There is no such thing as hate speech. There is no such thing as hate speech. There is no such thing as hate speech. There is no such thing as hate speech. There is no such thing as hate speech. There is no such thing as hate speech. There is no such thing as hate speech. There is no such thing as hate speech. There is no such thing as hate speech.

There is no such thing as hate speech. There is no such thing as hate speech. There is no such thing as hate speech. There is no such thing as hate speech. There is no such thing as hate speech.

...there is no such thing as hate speech.

There is no such thing as hate speech.
There is no such thing as
hate speech. There
is no such thing as hate,
speech.

There is no such
thing as hate speech. There is no
such thing as hate speech. There is
no such thing as hate,
speech.

There is no such thing as hate,
speech. There is no such
thing as hate speech. There is no such,
thing as hate
speech. There is no such thing as
hate speech.

There
is no such thing
as hate speech. There is
no such thing, as hate speech.

There is no such thing as hate speech. There is no such thing as hate speech. There is no such thing as hate speech. There is no such thing as hate speech. There is no such thing as hate speech. There is no such thing as hate speech. There is no such thing as hate speech. There is no such thing as hate speech. There is no such thing as hate speech. There is no such thing as hate speech. There is no such thing as hate speech.

There is no such thing as hate speech. There is no such thing as hate speech. There is no such thing as hate speech. There is no such thing as hate speech. There is no such thing as hate speech. There is no such thing as hate speech. There is no such thing as hate speech.

There is no such thing as hate speech. There is no such thing as hate speech. There is no such thing as hate speech. There is no such thing as hate speech. There is no such thing as hate speech. There is no such thing as hate speech. There is no such thing as hate speech. There is no such thing as hate speech.

There is no such thing as hate speech. There is no such thing as hate speech. There is no such thing as hate speech. There is no such thing as hate speech. There is no such thing as hate speech. There is no such thing as hate speech. There is no such thing as hate speech. There is no such thing as hate speech. There is no such thing as hate speech. There is no such thing as hate speech. There is no such thing as hate speech.

There is no such thing as hate speech. There is no such thing as hate speech. There is no such thing as hate speech. There is no such thing as hate speech. There is no such thing as

hate speech. There is no such thing as hate speech. There is no such thing as hate speech. There is no such thing as hate speech. There is no such thing as hate speech. There is no such thing as hate speech. There is no such thing as hate speech. There is no such thing as hate speech. There is no such thing as hate speech. There is no such thing as hate speech. There is no such thing as hate speech. There is no such thing as hate speech. There is no such thing as hate speech. There is no such thing as hate speech. There is no such thing as hate speech.

There is no such thing as hate speech.
There is no such thing as
hate speech. There
is no such thing as hate,
speech.
There is no such
thing as hate speech. There is no

such thing as hate speech. There is
no such thing as hate,
speech.

There is no such thing as hate,
speech. There is no such
thing as hate speech. There is no such, thing
as hate speech. There is
no such thing as hate speech. There
is no such thing
as hate speech. There is
no such thing,
as hate speech.

There is no such thing as hate speech. There is no such thing as hate speech. There is no such thing as hate speech. There is no such thing as hate speech. There is no such thing as hate speech. There is no such thing as hate speech. There is no such thing as hate speech. There is no such thing as hate speech. There is

no such thing as hate speech. There is no such thing as hate speech.

There is no such thing as hate speech. There is no such thing as hate speech. There is no such thing as hate speech. There is no such thing as hate speech. There is no such thing as hate speech. There is no such thing as hate speech. There is no such thing as hate speech. There is no such thing as hate speech. There is no such thing as hate speech. There is no such thing as hate speech. There is no such thing as hate speech.

There is no such thing as hate speech. There is no such thing as hate speech. There is no such thing as hate speech. There is no such thing as hate speech. There is no such thing as hate speech. There is no such thing as hate speech. There is no such thing as hate speech. There is no such thing as hate speech. There is no such thing as hate speech. There is no such thing as hate speech. There is no such thing as

hate speech. There is no such thing as hate speech.

There is no such thing as hate speech. There is no such thing as hate speech. There is no such thing as hate speech. There is no such thing as hate speech. There is no such thing as hate speech. There is no such thing as hate speech. There is no such thing as hate speech. There is no such thing as hate speech. There is no such thing as hate speech. There is no such thing as hate speech. There is no such thing as hate speech. There is no such thing as hate speech. There is no such thing as hate speech. There is no such thing as hate speech.

There is no such thing as hate speech. There is no such thing as hate speech. There is no such thing as hate speech. There is no such thing as hate speech. There is no such thing as hate speech. There is no such thing as hate

speech. There is no such thing as hate speech. There is no such thing as hate speech. There is no such thing as hate speech. There is no such thing as hate speech. There is no such thing as hate speech. There is no such thing as hate speech.

15

Speaking Truth to Power

There is no such thing as hate speech. There is no such thing as hate speech. There is no such thing as hate speech. There is no such thing as hate speech. There is no such thing as hate speech. There is no such thing as hate speech. There is no such thing as hate speech. There is no such thing as hate speech. There is no such thing as hate speech.

There is no such thing as hate speech. There is no such thing as hate speech. There is no such thing as hate speech. There is no such thing as hate speech. There is no such thing as

hate speech. There is no such thing as hate speech. There is no such thing as hate speech. There is no such thing as hate speech. There is no such thing as hate speech.

There is no such thing as hate speech. There is no such thing as hate speech. There is no such thing as hate speech. There is no such thing as hate speech. There is no such thing as hate speech. There is no such thing as hate speech. There is no such thing as hate speech. There is no such thing as hate speech. There is no such thing as hate speech. There is no such thing as hate speech.

There is no such thing as hate speech. There is no such thing as hate speech. There is no such thing as hate speech. There is no such thing as hate speech. There is no such thing as hate speech. There is no such thing as hate speech. There is no such thing as hate speech.

There is no such thing as hate speech.

There is no such thing as hate speech. There is no such thing as hate speech. There is no such thing as hate speech.

There is no such thing as hate speech. There is no such thing as hate speech. There is no such thing as hate speech. There is no such thing as hate speech. There is no such thing as hate speech. There is no such thing as hate speech. There is no such thing as hate speech. There is no such thing as hate speech.

There is no such thing as hate speech. There is no such thing as hate speech. There is no such thing as hate speech. There is no such thing as hate speech. There is no such thing as hate speech. There is no such thing as hate speech. There is no such thing as hate speech. There is no such thing as hate speech. There is no such thing as hate speech. There is no such thing as hate speech. There is no such thing as hate speech. There is no such thing as hate speech. There is no such thing as hate speech.

There is no such thing as hate speech. There is no such thing as hate speech.

There is no such thing as hate speech. There is no such thing as hate speech. There is no such thing as hate speech. There is no such thing as hate speech. There is no such thing as hate speech. There is no such thing as hate speech. There is no such thing as hate speech. There is no such thing as hate speech. There is no such thing as hate speech. There is no such thing as hate speech. There is no such thing as hate speech.

There is no such thing as hate speech. There is no such thing as hate speech. There is no such thing as hate speech. There is no such thing as hate speech. There is no such thing as hate speech. There is no such thing as hate speech. There is no such thing as hate speech. There is no such thing as hate speech. There is no such thing as hate speech. There is no such thing as hate speech. There is no such thing as

hate speech. There is no such thing as hate speech. There is no such thing as hate speech. There is no such thing as hate speech. There is no such thing as hate speech. There is no such thing as hate speech. There is no such thing as hate speech. There is no such thing as hate speech. There is no such thing as hate speech. There is no such thing as hate speech.

There is no such thing as hate speech. There is no such thing as hate speech. There is no such thing as hate speech. There is no such thing as hate speech. There is no such thing as hate speech. There is no such thing as hate speech. There is no such thing as hate speech. There is no such thing as hate speech. There is no such thing as hate speech. There is no such thing as hate speech.

There is no such thing as hate speech. There is no such thing as hate speech. There is no such thing as hate speech. There is no such thing as hate speech. There is no such thing as

hate speech. There is no such thing as hate speech. There is no such thing as hate speech. There is no such thing as hate speech. There is no such thing as hate speech. There is no such thing as hate speech. There is no such thing as hate speech. There is no such thing as hate speech. There is no such thing as hate speech. There is no such thing as hate speech. There is no such thing as hate speech. There is no such thing as hate speech. There is no such thing as hate speech. There is no such thing as hate speech. There is no such thing as hate speech. There is no such thing as hate speech. There is no such thing as hate speech. There is no such thing as hate speech. There is no such thing as hate speech.

There is no such thing as hate speech. There is no such thing as hate speech. There is no such thing as hate speech. There is no such thing as hate speech. There is no such thing as hate speech. There is no such thing as hate

speech. There is no such thing as hate speech. There is no such thing as hate speech. There is no such thing as hate speech. There is no such thing as hate speech. There is no such thing as hate speech. There is no such thing as hate speech. There is no such thing as hate speech. There is no such thing as hate speech. There is no such thing as hate speech. There is no such thing as hate speech.

There is no such thing as hate speech. There is no such thing as hate speech. There is no such thing as hate speech. There is no such thing as hate speech. There is no such thing as hate speech. There is no such thing as hate speech. There is no such thing as hate speech. There is no such thing as hate speech. There is no such thing as hate speech. There is no such thing as hate speech. There is no such thing as hate speech. There is no such thing as hate speech.

16

My Words, My Song

There is no such thing as hate speech. There is no such thing as hate speech. There is no such thing as hate speech. There is no such thing as hate speech. There is no such thing as hate speech. There is no such thing as hate speech. There is no such thing as hate speech. There is no such thing as hate speech. There is no such thing as hate speech.

There is no such thing as hate speech. There is no such thing as hate speech. There is no such thing as hate speech. There is no such thing as hate speech. There is no such thing as hate speech. There is no such thing as hate speech. There is no such thing as hate speech.

There is no such thing as hate speech. There is no such thing as hate speech.

There is no such thing as hate speech. There is no such thing as hate speech. There is no such thing as hate speech. There is no such thing as hate speech. There is no such thing as hate speech. There is no such thing as hate speech. There is no such thing as hate speech. There is no such thing as hate speech. There is no such thing as hate speech. There is no such thing as hate speech. There is no such thing as hate speech.

There is no such thing as hate speech. There is no such thing as hate speech. There is no such thing as hate speech. There is no such thing as hate speech. There is no such thing as hate speech. There is no such thing as hate speech. There is no such thing as hate speech. There is no such thing as hate speech. There is no such thing as hate speech. There is no such

...there is no
such thing as
hate speech...

thing as hate speech. There is no such thing as hate speech. There is no such thing as hate speech.

There is no such thing as hate speech. There is no such thing as hate speech. There is no such thing as hate speech. There is no such thing as hate speech. There is no such thing as hate speech. There is no such thing as hate speech. There is no such thing as hate speech. There is no such thing as hate speech.

There is no such thing as hate speech. There is no such thing as hate speech. There is no such thing as hate speech. There is no such thing as hate speech. There is no such thing as hate speech. There is no such thing as hate speech. There is no such thing as hate speech. There is no such thing as hate speech. There is no such thing as hate speech. There is no such thing as hate speech. There is no such thing as hate speech. There is no such thing as hate speech.

There is no such thing as hate speech. There is no such thing as hate speech.

There is no such thing as hate speech. There is no such thing as hate speech. There is no such thing as hate speech. There is no such thing as hate speech. There is no such thing as hate speech. There is no such thing as hate speech. There is no such thing as hate speech. There is no such thing as hate speech. There is no such thing as hate speech. There is no such thing as hate speech. There is no such thing as hate speech.

There is no such thing as hate speech. There is no such thing as hate speech. There is no such thing as hate speech. There is no such thing as hate speech. There is no such thing as hate speech. There is no such thing as hate speech. There is no such thing as hate speech. There is no such thing as hate speech. There is no such thing as hate speech. There is no such thing as

hate speech. There is no such thing as hate speech. There is no such thing as hate speech. There is no such thing as hate speech. There is no such thing as hate speech. There is no such thing as hate speech. There is no such thing as hate speech. There is no such thing as hate speech. There is no such thing as hate speech. There is no such thing as hate speech.

There is no such thing as hate speech. There is no such thing as hate speech. There is no such thing as hate speech. There is no such thing as hate speech. There is no such thing as hate speech. There is no such thing as hate speech. There is no such thing as hate speech. There is no such thing as hate speech. There is no such thing as hate speech. There is no such thing as hate speech.

There is no such thing as hate speech. There is no such thing as hate speech. There is no such thing as hate speech. There is no such thing as hate speech. There is no such thing as

hate speech. There is no such thing as hate speech. There is no such thing as hate speech. There is no such thing as hate speech. There is no such thing as hate speech. There is no such thing as hate speech. There is no such thing as hate speech. There is no such thing as hate speech. There is no such thing as hate speech. There is no such thing as hate speech. There is no such thing as hate speech. There is no such thing as hate speech. There is no such thing as hate speech. There is no such thing as hate speech. There is no such thing as hate speech. There is no such thing as hate speech. There is no such thing as hate speech. There is no such thing as hate speech. There is no such thing as hate speech.

There is no such thing as hate speech. There is no such thing as hate speech. There is no such thing as hate speech. There is no such thing as hate speech. There is no such thing as hate speech. There is no such thing as hate

speech. There is no such thing as hate speech. There is no such thing as hate speech. There is no such thing as hate speech. There is no such thing as hate speech. There is no such thing as hate speech. There is no such thing as hate speech. There is no such thing as hate speech. There is no such thing as hate speech. There is no such thing as hate speech. There is no such thing as hate speech.

There is no such thing as hate speech. There is no such thing as hate speech. There is no such thing as hate speech. There is no such thing as hate speech. There is no such thing as hate speech. There is no such thing as hate speech. There is no such thing as hate speech. There is no such thing as hate speech. There is no such thing as hate speech. There is no such thing as hate speech. There is no such thing as hate speech. There is no such thing as hate speech. There is no such thing as hate speech.

17

What She Said to Me

There is no such thing as hate speech. There is no such thing as hate speech. There is no such thing as hate speech.

There is no such thing as hate speech. There is no such thing as hate speech. There is no such thing as hate speech. There is no such thing as hate speech. There is no such thing as hate speech. There is no such thing as hate speech.

There is no such thing as hate speech. There is no such thing as hate speech. There is no such thing as hate speech. There is no such thing as hate speech. There is no such thing as hate speech. There is no such thing as hate

speech. There is no such thing as hate speech. There is no such thing as hate speech. There is no such thing as hate speech.

There is no such thing as hate speech. There is no such thing as hate speech. There is no such thing as hate speech. There is no such thing as hate speech. There is no such thing as hate speech. There is no such thing as hate speech. There is no such thing as hate speech. There is no such thing as hate speech. There is no such thing as hate speech. There is no such thing as hate speech. There is no such thing as hate speech.

There is no such thing as hate speech. There is no such thing as hate speech. There is no such thing as hate speech. There is no such thing as hate speech. There is no such thing as hate speech. There is no such thing as hate speech. There is no such thing as hate speech. There is no such thing as hate speech. There is no such thing as hate speech. There is no such

There is no
such thing...as
hate speech.

thing as hate speech. There is no such thing as hate speech. There is no such thing as hate speech.

There is no such thing as hate speech. There is no such thing as hate speech. There is no such thing as hate speech. There is no such thing as hate speech. There is no such thing as hate speech. There is no such thing as hate speech. There is no such thing as hate speech. There is no such thing as hate speech.

There is no such thing as hate speech. There is no such thing as hate speech. There is no such thing as hate speech. There is no such thing as hate speech. There is no such thing as hate speech. There is no such thing as hate speech. There is no such thing as hate speech. There is no such thing as hate speech. There is no such thing as hate speech. There is no such thing as hate speech. There is no such thing as hate speech. There is no such thing as hate speech. There is no such thing as hate speech. There is no such thing as hate speech.

There is no such thing as hate speech. There is no such thing as hate speech.

There is no such thing as hate speech. There is no such thing as hate speech. There is no such thing as hate speech. There is no such thing as hate speech. There is no such thing as hate speech. There is no such thing as hate speech. There is no such thing as hate speech. There is no such thing as hate speech. There is no such thing as hate speech. There is no such thing as hate speech. There is no such thing as hate speech.

There is no such thing as hate speech. There is no such thing as hate speech. There is no such thing as hate speech. There is no such thing as hate speech. There is no such thing as hate speech. There is no such thing as hate speech. There is no such thing as hate speech. There is no such thing as hate speech. There is no such thing as hate speech. There is no such thing as hate speech. There is no such thing as

hate speech. There is no such thing as hate speech. There is no such thing as hate speech. There is no such thing as hate speech. There is no such thing as hate speech. There is no such thing as hate speech. There is no such thing as hate speech. There is no such thing as hate speech. There is no such thing as hate speech. There is no such thing as hate speech.

There is no such thing as hate speech. There is no such thing as hate speech. There is no such thing as hate speech. There is no such thing as hate speech. There is no such thing as hate speech. There is no such thing as hate speech. There is no such thing as hate speech. There is no such thing as hate speech. There is no such thing as hate speech. There is no such thing as hate speech.

There is no such thing as hate speech. There is no such thing as hate speech. There is no such thing as hate speech. There is no such thing as hate speech. There is no such thing as

hate speech. There is no such thing as hate speech. There is no such thing as hate speech. There is no such thing as hate speech. There is no such thing as hate speech. There is no such thing as hate speech. There is no such thing as hate speech. There is no such thing as hate speech. There is no such thing as hate speech. There is no such thing as hate speech. There is no such thing as hate speech. There is no such thing as hate speech. There is no such thing as hate speech. There is no such thing as hate speech. There is no such thing as hate speech. There is no such thing as hate speech. There is no such thing as hate speech. There is no such thing as hate speech. There is no such thing as hate speech.

There is no such thing as hate speech. There is no such thing as hate speech. There is no such thing as hate speech. There is no such thing as hate speech. There is no such thing as hate speech. There is no such thing as hate

speech. There is no such thing as hate speech. There is no such thing as hate speech. There is no such thing as hate speech. There is no such thing as hate speech. There is no such thing as hate speech. There is no such thing as hate speech. There is no such thing as hate speech. There is no such thing as hate speech. There is no such thing as hate speech. There is no such thing as hate speech.

There is no such thing as hate speech. There is no such thing as hate speech. There is no such thing as hate speech. There is no such thing as hate speech. There is no such thing as hate speech. There is no such thing as hate speech. There is no such thing as hate speech. There is no such thing as hate speech. There is no such thing as hate speech. There is no such thing as hate speech. There is no such thing as hate speech. There is no such thing as hate speech. There is no such thing as hate speech.

18

Speech that Dances

There is no such thing as hate speech. There is no such thing as hate speech. There is no such thing as hate speech. There is no such thing as hate speech. There is no such thing as hate speech. There is no such thing as hate speech. There is no such thing as hate speech. There is no such thing as hate speech. There is no such thing as hate speech.

There is no such thing as hate speech. There is no such thing as hate speech. There is no such thing as hate speech. There is no such thing as hate speech. There is no such thing as hate speech. There is no such thing as hate speech.

There is no such thing as hate speech. There is no such thing as hate speech.

There is no such thing as hate speech. There is no such thing as hate speech. There is no such thing as hate speech. There is no such thing as hate speech. There is no such thing as hate speech. There is no such thing as hate speech. There is no such thing as hate speech. There is no such thing as hate speech. There is no such thing as hate speech. There is no such thing as hate speech. There is no such thing as hate speech.

There is no such thing as hate speech. There is no such thing as hate speech. There is no such thing as hate speech. There is no such thing as hate speech. There is no such thing as hate speech. There is no such thing as hate speech. There is no such thing as hate speech. There is no such thing as hate speech. There is no such thing as hate speech.

There is no such thing as hate speech.

There is no such thing as hate speech.
There is no such thing as
hate speech. There
is no such thing as hate,
speech.
There is no such
thing as hate speech.

There is no
such thing as hate speech. There is
no such thing as hate,
speech.

There is no such thing as hate,
speech. There is no such
thing as hate speech.
There is no such, thing as hate speech.
There is no such thing as hate speech. There
is no such thing
as hate speech. There is
no such thing,

as hate speech.
There is no such thing as hate speech.
There is no such thing as
hate speech. There
is no such
thing as hate,
speech.

There is no such
thing as hate speech. There is no
such thing as hate speech. There is
no such thing as hate,
speech.

There is no such thing as hate,
speech. There is no such
thing as hate speech. There is no such, thing
as hate speech. There is
no such thing as hate speech.

There is no such thing
as hate speech. There is no such thing,
as hate speech.
There is no such thing as hate speech.
There is no such thing as
hate speech. There
is no such thing as hate speech.

There is no such
thing as hate speech. There is no
such thing as hate speech. There is
no such thing as hate,
speech.

There is no such thing as hate,
speech. There is no such
thing as hate speech. There is no such, thing
as hate speech. There is
no such thing as hate speech.

There is no such thing
as hate speech. There is no such thing,
as hate speech.

There is no such thing as hate speech. There is no such thing as hate speech. There is no such thing as hate speech.
There is no such thing as hate speech. There is no such thing as hate speech. There is no such thing as hate speech. There is no such thing as hate speech. There is no such thing as hate speech. There is no such thing as hate speech. There is no such thing as hate speech. There is no such thing as hate speech.

There is no such thing as hate speech. There is no such thing as hate speech. There is no such thing as hate speech. There is no such thing as hate speech. There is no such thing as hate speech. There is no such thing as hate speech. There is no such thing as hate speech.

There is no such thing as hate speech. There is no such thing as hate speech. There is no such thing as hate speech. There is no such thing as hate speech. There is no such thing as hate speech. There is no such thing as hate speech. There is no such thing as hate speech. There is no such thing as hate speech.

There is no such thing as hate speech. There is no such thing as hate speech. There is no such thing as hate speech. There is no such thing as hate speech. There is no such thing as hate speech. There is no such thing as hate speech. There is no such thing as hate speech. There is no such thing as hate speech. There is no such thing as hate speech. There is no such thing as hate speech. There is no such thing as hate speech.

There is no such thing as hate speech. There is no such thing as hate speech. There is no such thing as hate speech. There is no such thing as hate speech. There is no such thing as

hate speech. There is no such thing as hate speech. There is no such thing as hate speech. There is no such thing as hate speech. There is no such thing as hate speech. There is no such thing as hate speech. There is no such thing as hate speech. There is no such thing as hate speech. There is no such thing as hate speech. There is no such thing as hate speech. There is no such thing as hate speech. There is no such thing as hate speech. There is no such thing as hate speech. There is no such thing as hate speech. There is no such thing as hate speech.

There is no such thing as hate speech. There is no such thing as hate speech. There is no such thing as hate speech. There is no such thing as hate speech. There is no such thing as hate speech. There is no such thing as hate speech. There is no such thing as hate speech. There is no such thing as hate speech. There is

no such thing as hate speech. There is no such thing as hate speech.

There is no such thing as hate speech. There is no such thing as hate speech. There is no such thing as hate speech. There is no such thing as hate speech. There is no such thing as hate speech. There is no such thing as hate speech. There is no such thing as hate speech. There is no such thing as hate speech. There is no such thing as hate speech. There is no such thing as hate speech. There is no such thing as hate speech. There is no such thing as hate speech. There is no such thing as hate speech. There is no such thing as hate speech. There is no such thing as hate speech. There is no such thing as hate speech. There is no such thing as hate speech. There is no such thing as hate speech. There is no such thing as hate speech. There is no such

thing as hate speech. There is no such thing as hate speech.

There is no such thing as hate speech. There is no such thing as hate speech. There is no such thing as hate speech. There is no such thing as hate speech. There is no such thing as hate speech. There is no such thing as hate speech. There is no such thing as hate speech. There is no such thing as hate speech. There is no such thing as hate speech. There is no such thing as hate speech. There is no such thing as hate speech. There is no such thing as hate speech. There is no such thing as hate speech. There is no such thing as hate speech. There is no such thing as hate speech.

There is no such thing as hate speech. There is no such thing as hate speech. There is no such thing as hate speech. There is no such thing as hate speech. There is no such thing as hate speech. There is no such thing as hate

speech. There is no such thing as hate speech. There is no such thing as hate speech. There is no such thing as hate speech. There is no such thing as hate speech. There is no such thing as hate speech. There is no such thing as hate speech.

19

Alone with Your Words

There is no such thing as hate speech. There is no such thing as hate speech. There is no such thing as hate speech. There is no such thing as hate speech. There is no such thing as hate speech. There is no such thing as hate speech. There is no such thing as hate speech. There is no such thing as hate speech. There is no such thing as hate speech.

There is no such thing as hate speech. There is no such thing as hate speech. There is no such thing as hate speech. There is no such thing as hate speech. There is no such thing as

hate speech. There is no such thing as hate speech. There is no such thing as hate speech. There is no such thing as hate speech. There is no such thing as hate speech.

There is no such thing as hate speech. There is no such thing as hate speech. There is no such thing as hate speech. There is no such thing as hate speech. There is no such thing as hate speech. There is no such thing as hate speech. There is no such thing as hate speech. There is no such thing as hate speech. There is no such thing as hate speech. There is no such thing as hate speech. There is no such thing as hate speech.

There is no such thing as hate speech. There is no such thing as hate speech. There is no such thing as hate speech. There is no such thing as hate speech. There is no such thing as hate speech. There is no such thing as hate speech. There is no such thing as hate speech.

There is no
such thing as
hate speech

There is no such thing as hate speech. There is no such thing as hate speech. There is no such thing as hate speech.

"There is no such thing", as hate speech. There is no such, thing as hate speech!"

"There is no such thing as hate speech. There is no such thing."

"As hate speech. There is no such thing as hate speech. There is no such thing as hate speech. There is,"

"…no such thing as hate speech. There is no such thing as hate speech. There…Is no such thing as hate speech!"

There is no such thing as hate speech. There is no such thing as hate speech. There is no such thing as hate speech. There is no such thing as hate speech. There is no such thing as hate speech. There is no such thing as hate speech. There is no such thing as hate speech. There is no such thing as hate speech.

There is no such thing as hate speech. There is no such thing as hate speech. There is no such thing as hate speech. There is no such thing as hate speech. There is no such thing as hate speech. There is no such thing as hate speech. There is no such thing as hate speech. There is no such thing as hate speech. There is no such thing as hate speech. There is no such thing as hate speech. There is no such thing as hate speech. There is no such thing as hate speech. There is no such thing as hate speech. There is no such thing as hate speech.

"There is no such thing", as hate speech. There is no such,"

"Thing as hate speech!"

"There is no such thing as hate speech. There is no such thing. As hate speech. There is no such thing as hate speech. There is no such thing as hate speech. There is,"

"…no such thing as hate speech. There is no such thing as hate speech."

"There is no such thing as hate speech!"

There is no such thing as hate speech. There is no such thing as hate speech. There is no such thing as hate speech. There is no such thing as hate speech. There is no such thing as hate speech. There is no such thing as hate speech. There is no such thing as hate speech. There is no such thing as hate speech. There is no such thing as hate speech. There is no such thing as hate speech. There is no such thing as hate speech.

"There is no such thing", as hate speech. There is no such, thing as hate speech!"

"There is no such thing as hate speech. There is no such thing."

"As hate speech."

"There is no such thing as hate speech. There is no such thing as hate speech."

"There is no such thing as hate speech."

"There is no such thing as hate speech. "There…Is no such thing as hate speech!"

There is no such thing as hate speech. There is no such thing as hate speech. There is no such thing as hate speech. There is no such thing as hate speech. There is no such thing as hate speech. There is no such thing as hate speech. There is no such thing as hate speech. There is no such thing as hate speech. There is no such thing as hate speech. There is no such thing as hate speech. There is no such thing as hate speech. There is no such thing as hate speech. There is no such thing as hate speech. There is no such thing as hate speech. There is no such thing as hate speech. There is no such thing as hate speech. There is no such thing as hate speech. There is no such thing as hate speech.

There is no such thing as hate speech. There is no such thing as hate speech. There is

no such thing as hate speech. There is no such thing as hate speech. There is no such thing as hate speech. There is no such thing as hate speech. There is no such thing as hate speech. There is no such thing as hate speech. There is no such thing as hate speech. There is no such thing as hate speech.

"There is…"

"…no such thing", as hate speech. There is no such, thing as hate speech!"

"There is no such thing as hate speech. There is no such thing."

"As hate speech. There is no,"

"Such thing as hate speech. There is no such thing as hate speech. There is,"

"…no such thing as hate speech. There is no such thing as hate speech. There…Is no such thing as hate speech!"

"There is no such thing", as hate speech. There is no such, thing as hate speech?"

"There is no such thing as hate speech. There is no such thing."
"As hate speech."
"There is no such thing as hate speech. There is no such thing as hate speech. There is,"
"No such thing as hate speech. There is no such thing as hate speech. There is no such thing as hate speech."

There is no such thing as hate speech. There is no such thing as hate speech. There is no such thing as hate speech. There is no such thing as hate speech. There is no such thing as hate speech. There is no such thing as hate speech. There is no such thing as hate speech. There is no such thing as hate speech. There is no such thing as hate speech. There is no such thing as hate speech. There is no such thing as hate speech. There is no such thing as hate speech. There is no such thing as hate speech. There is no such thing as hate speech. There is no such

thing as hate speech. There is no such thing as hate speech. There is no such thing as hate speech. There is no such thing as hate speech. There is no such thing as hate speech. There is no such thing as hate speech. There is no such thing as hate speech. There is no such thing as hate speech.

There is no such thing as hate speech. There is no such thing as hate speech. There is no such thing as hate speech. There is no such thing as hate speech. There is no such thing as hate speech. There is no such thing as hate speech. There is no such thing as hate speech. There is no such thing as hate speech. There is no such thing as hate speech. There is no such thing as hate speech. There is no such thing as hate speech. There is no such thing as hate speech. There is no such thing as hate speech. There is no such thing as hate speech. There is no such thing as hate speech.

There is no such thing as hate speech. There is no such thing as hate speech. There is no such thing as hate speech. There is no such thing as hate speech. There is no such thing as hate speech. There is no such thing as hate speech. There is no such thing as hate speech. There is no such thing as hate speech. There is no such thing as hate speech. There is no such thing as hate speech. There is no such thing as hate speech. There is no such thing as hate speech.

"There is no such thing", as hate speech. There is no such, thing as hate speech!"

"There is no such thing as hate speech. There is no such thing. As hate speech. There is no such thing as hate speech. There is no such thing as hate speech. There is no such thing as hate speech. There is no such thing as hate speech. There is no such thing as hate speech!"

20

If I Say This to You...

There is no such thing as hate speech. There is no such thing as hate speech. There is no such thing as hate speech. There is no such thing as hate speech.

There is no such thing as hate speech. There is no such thing as hate speech. There is no such thing as hate speech. There is no such thing as hate speech. There is no such thing as hate speech.

There is no such thing as hate speech. There is no such thing as hate speech. There is

no such thing as hate speech. There is no such thing as hate speech. There is no such thing as hate speech. There is no such thing as hate speech. There is no such thing as hate speech. There is no such thing as hate speech. There is no such thing as hate speech.

There is no such thing as hate speech. There is no such thing as hate speech. There is no such thing as hate speech. There is no such thing as hate speech. There is no such thing as hate speech. There is no such thing as hate speech. There is no such thing as hate speech. There is no such thing as hate speech. There is no such thing as hate speech. There is no such thing as hate speech. There is no such thing as hate speech.

There is no such thing as hate speech. There is no such thing as hate speech. There is no such thing as hate speech. There is no such thing as hate speech. There is no such thing as

There is no such
thing as hate
speech.

hate speech. There is no such thing as hate speech. There is no such thing as hate speech. There is no such thing as hate speech. There is no such thing as hate speech. There is no such

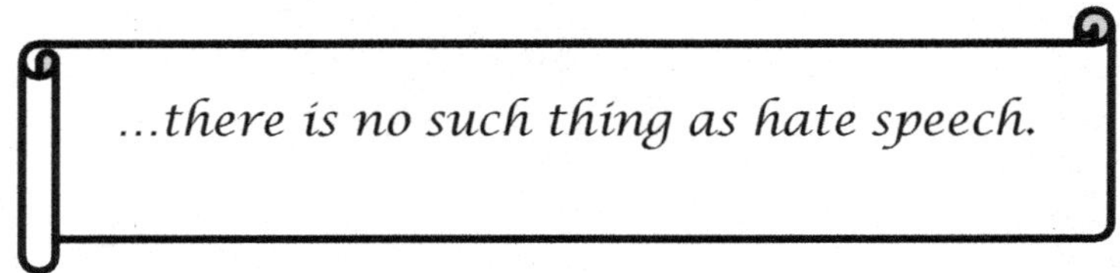

thing as hate speech. There is no such thing as hate speech. There is no such thing as hate speech.

There is no such thing as hate speech. There is no such thing as hate speech. There is no such thing as hate speech. There is no such thing as hate speech. There is no such thing as hate speech. There is no such thing as hate speech. There is no such thing as hate speech. There is no such thing as hate speech.

There is no such thing as hate speech. There is no such thing as hate speech. There is

no such thing as hate speech. There is no such thing as hate speech. There is no such thing as hate speech. There is no such thing as hate speech. There is no such thing as hate speech. There is no such thing as hate speech. There is no such thing as hate speech. There is no such thing as hate speech. There is no such thing as hate speech. There is no such thing as hate speech. There is no such thing as hate speech. There is no such thing as hate speech.

There is no such thing as hate speech. There is no such thing as hate speech. There is no such thing as hate speech. There is no such thing as hate speech. There is no such thing as hate speech.

There is no such thing as hate speech.

There is no such thing as hate speech. There is no such thing as hate speech. There is no such thing as hate speech. There is no such thing as hate speech.

There is no such thing as hate speech. There is no such thing as hate speech.

There is no such thing as hate speech. There is no such thing as hate speech. There is no such thing as hate speech. There is no such thing as hate speech. There is no such thing as hate speech. There is no such thing as hate speech. There is no such thing as hate speech. There is no such thing as hate speech. There is no such thing as hate speech. There is no such thing as hate speech.

There is no such thing as hate speech.
There is no such thing as...hate speech.

There is no such thing as hate speech. There is no such thing as hate speech. There is no such thing as hate speech. There is no such thing as hate speech. There is no such thing as hate speech. There is no such thing as hate speech. There is no such thing as hate speech. There is no such thing as hate speech. There is

no such thing as hate speech. There is no such thing as hate speech. There is no such thing as hate speech. There is no such thing as hate speech. There is no such thing as hate speech. There is no such thing as hate speech. There is no such thing as hate speech.

There is no such thing as hate speech. There is no such thing as hate speech. There is no such thing as hate speech. There is no such thing as hate speech. There is no such thing as hate speech. There is no such thing as hate speech. There is no such thing as hate speech. There is no such thing as hate speech.

There is no such thing as hate speech. There is no such thing as hate speech. There is no such thing as hate speech. There is no such thing as hate speech. There is no such thing as hate speech. There is no such thing as hate speech. There is no such thing as hate speech. There is no such thing as hate speech. There is no such thing as hate speech. There is no such

thing as hate speech. There is no such thing as hate speech. There is no such thing as hate speech. There is no such thing as hate speech. There is no such thing as hate speech. There is no such thing as hate speech. There is no such thing as hate speech.

There is no such thing as hate speech. There is no such thing as hate speech. There is no such thing as hate speech. There is no such thing as hate speech. There is no such thing as hate speech. There is no such thing as hate speech. There is no such thing as hate speech. There is no such thing as hate speech. There is no such thing as hate speech. There is no such thing as hate speech. There is no such thing as hate speech.

21

The Boy and His Words

There is no such thing as hate speech. There is no such thing as hate speech. There is no such thing as hate speech. There is no such thing as hate speech. There is no such thing as hate speech. There is no such thing as hate speech. There is no such thing as hate speech. There is no such thing as hate speech. There is no such thing as hate speech.

There is no such thing as hate speech. There is no such thing as hate speech. There is no such thing as hate speech. There is no such thing as hate speech. There is no such thing as

hate speech. There is no such thing as hate speech. There is no such thing as hate speech. There is no such thing as hate speech. There is no such thing as hate speech.

There is no such thing as hate speech. There is no such thing as hate speech. There is no such thing as hate speech. There is no such thing as hate speech. There is no such thing as hate speech. There is no such thing as hate speech. There is no such thing as hate speech. There is no such thing as hate speech. There is no such thing as hate speech. There is no such thing as hate speech. There is no such thing as hate speech.

There is no such thing as hate speech. There is no such thing as hate speech. There is no such thing as hate speech. There is no such thing as hate speech. There is no such thing as hate speech. There is no such thing as hate speech. There is no such thing as hate speech.

...there is no
such thing as
hate speech.

There is no such thing as hate speech. There is no such thing as hate speech. There is no such thing as hate speech.

There is no such thing as hate speech. There is no such thing as hate speech. There is no such thing as hate speech. There is no such thing as hate speech. There is no such thing as hate speech. There is no such thing as hate speech. There is no such thing as hate speech. There is no such thing as hate speech.

There is no such thing as hate speech. There is no such thing as hate speech. There is no such thing as hate speech. There is no such thing as hate speech. There is no such thing as hate speech. There is no such thing as hate speech. There is no such thing as hate speech. There is no such thing as hate speech. There is no such thing as hate speech. There is no such thing as hate speech. There is no such thing as hate speech. There is no such thing as hate speech. There is no such thing as hate speech.

There is no such thing as hate speech. There is no such thing as hate speech.

There is no such thing as hate speech. There is no such thing as hate speech. There is no such thing as hate speech. There is no such thing as hate speech. There is no such thing as hate speech. There is no such thing as hate speech. There is no such thing as hate speech. There is no such thing as hate speech. There is no such thing as hate speech. There is no such thing as hate speech. There is no such thing as hate speech.

There is no such thing as hate speech. There is no such thing as hate speech. There is no such thing as hate speech. There is no such thing as hate speech. There is no such thing as hate speech. There is no such thing as hate speech. There is no such thing as hate speech. There is no such thing as hate speech. There is no such thing as hate speech. There is no such thing as hate speech. There is no such thing as

hate speech. There is no such thing as hate speech. There is no such thing as hate speech. There is no such thing as hate speech. There is no such thing as hate speech. There is no such thing as hate speech. There is no such thing as hate speech. There is no such thing as hate speech. There is no such thing as hate speech. There is no such thing as hate speech.

There is no such thing as hate speech. There is no such thing as hate speech. There is no such thing as hate speech. There is no such thing as hate speech. There is no such thing as hate speech. There is no such thing as hate speech. There is no such thing as hate speech. There is no such thing as hate speech. There is no such thing as hate speech. There is no such thing as hate speech.

There is no such thing as hate speech. There is no such thing as hate speech. There is no such thing as hate speech. There is no such thing as hate speech. There is no such thing as

hate speech. There is no such thing as hate speech. There is no such thing as hate speech. There is no such thing as hate speech. There is no such thing as hate speech. There is no such thing as hate speech. There is no such thing as hate speech. There is no such thing as hate speech. There is no such thing as hate speech. There is no such thing as hate speech. There is no such thing as hate speech. There is no such thing as hate speech. There is no such thing as hate speech. There is no such thing as hate speech. There is no such thing as hate speech. There is no such thing as hate speech. There is no such thing as hate speech. There is no such thing as hate speech. There is no such thing as hate speech.

There is no such thing as hate speech. There is no such thing as hate speech. There is no such thing as hate speech. There is no such thing as hate speech. There is no such thing as hate speech. There is no such thing as hate

speech. There is no such thing as hate speech. There is no such thing as hate speech. There is no such thing as hate speech. There is no such thing as hate speech. There is no such thing as hate speech. There is no such thing as hate speech. There is no such thing as hate speech. There is no such thing as hate speech. There is no such thing as hate speech. There is no such thing as hate speech.

There is no such thing as hate speech. There is no such thing as hate speech. There is no such thing as hate speech. There is no such thing as hate speech. There is no such thing as hate speech. There is no such thing as hate speech. There is no such thing as hate speech. There is no such thing as hate speech. There is no such thing as hate speech. There is no such thing as hate speech. There is no such thing as hate speech. There is no such thing as hate speech.

22

If I Could Tell You My Words

There is no such thing as hate speech. There is no such thing as hate speech. There is no such thing as hate speech. There is no such thing as hate speech. There is no such thing as hate speech. There is no such thing as hate speech. There is no such thing as hate speech. There is no such thing as hate speech. There is no such thing as hate speech.

There is no such thing as hate speech. There is no such thing as hate speech. There is no such thing as hate speech. There is no such thing as hate speech. There is no such thing as

hate speech. There is no such thing as hate speech. There is no such thing as hate speech. There is no such thing as hate speech. There is no such thing as hate speech.

There is no such thing as hate speech. There is no such thing as hate speech. There is no such thing as hate speech. There is no such thing as hate speech. There is no such thing as hate speech. There is no such thing as hate speech. There is no such thing as hate speech. There is no such thing as hate speech. There is no such thing as hate speech. There is no such thing as hate speech.

There is no such thing as hate speech. There is no such thing as hate speech. There is no such thing as hate speech. There is no such thing as hate speech. There is no such thing as hate speech. There is no such thing as hate speech. There is no such thing as hate speech.

There is no such thing as hate speech.

There is no such thing as hate speech. There is no such thing as hate speech. There is no such thing as hate speech.

There is no such thing as hate speech.
There is no such thing as
hate speech. There
is no such thing as hate,
speech.
There is no such
thing as hate speech. There is no
such thing as hate speech. There is
no such thing as hate,
speech. There is no such thing as hate,
speech. There is no such
thing as hate speech. There is no such, thing
as hate speech. There is
no such thing as hate speech. There
is no such thing
as hate speech. There is
no such thing as hate speech.

There is no such thing as hate speech. There is no such thing as hate speech. There is no such thing as hate speech. There is no such thing as hate speech. There is no such thing as hate speech. There is no such thing as hate speech. There is no such thing as hate speech. There is no such thing as hate speech.

There is no such thing as hate speech. There is no such thing as hate speech. There is no such thing as hate speech. There is no such thing as hate speech. There is no such thing as hate speech. There is no such thing as hate speech. There is no such thing as hate speech. There is no such thing as hate speech. There is no such thing as hate speech. There is no such thing as hate speech. There is no such thing as hate speech. There is no such thing as hate speech. There is no such thing as hate speech. There is no such thing as hate speech.

There is no such thing as hate speech. There is no such thing as hate speech. There is no such thing as hate speech. There is no such thing as hate speech. There is no such thing as hate speech. There is no such thing as hate speech. There is no such thing as hate speech. There is no such thing as hate speech. There is no such thing as hate speech. There is no such thing as hate speech. There is no such thing as hate speech.

There is no such thing as hate speech. There is no such thing as hate speech. There is no such thing as hate speech. There is no such thing as hate speech. There is no such thing as hate speech. There is no such thing as hate speech. There is no such thing as hate speech. There is no such thing as hate speech. There is no such thing as hate speech. There is no such thing as hate speech. There is no such thing as hate speech. There is no such thing as hate speech. There is no such thing as hate speech.

There is no such thing as hate speech. There is no such thing as hate speech. There is no such thing as hate speech. There is no such thing as hate speech. There is no such thing as hate speech. There is no such thing as hate speech. There is no such thing as hate speech.

There is no such thing as hate speech. There is no such thing as hate speech. There is no such thing as hate speech. There is no such thing as hate speech. There is no such thing as hate speech. There is no such thing as hate speech. There is no such thing as hate speech. There is no such thing as hate speech. There is no such thing as hate speech. There is no such thing as hate speech.

There is no such thing as hate speech. There is no such thing as hate speech. There is no such thing as hate speech. There is no such thing as hate speech. There is no such thing as hate speech. There is no such thing as hate speech. There is no such thing as hate speech.

There is no such thing as hate speech. There is no such thing as hate speech. There is no such thing as hate speech. There is no such thing as hate speech. There is no such thing as hate speech. There is no such thing as hate speech. There is no such thing as hate speech. There is no such thing as hate speech. There is no such thing as hate speech. There is no such thing as hate speech. There is no such thing as hate speech. There is no such thing as hate speech. There is no such thing as hate speech. There is no such thing as hate speech. There is no such thing as hate speech. There is no such thing as hate speech.

There is no such thing as hate speech. There is no such thing as hate speech. There is no such thing as hate speech. There is no such thing as hate speech. There is no such thing as hate speech. There is no such thing as hate speech. There is no such thing as hate speech. There is no such thing as hate speech. There is

no such thing as hate speech. There is no such thing as hate speech. There is no such thing as hate speech. There is no such thing as hate speech. There is no such thing as hate speech. There is no such thing as hate speech. There is no such thing as hate speech. There is no such thing as hate speech.

There is no such thing as hate speech. There is no such thing as hate speech. There is no such thing as hate speech. There is no such thing as hate speech. There is no such thing as hate speech. There is no such thing as hate speech. There is no such thing as hate speech. There is no such thing as hate speech. There is no such thing as hate speech. There is no such thing as hate speech. There is no such thing as hate speech. There is no such thing as hate speech.

23

Do My Words Hurt More Than Yours?

There is no such thing as hate speech. There is no such thing as hate speech. There is no such thing as hate speech. There is no such thing as hate speech. There is no such thing as hate speech. There is no such thing as hate speech. There is no such thing as hate speech. There is no such thing as hate speech. There is no such thing as hate speech.

There is no such thing as hate speech. There is no such thing as hate speech. There is no such thing as hate speech. There is no such thing as hate speech. There is no such thing as

hate speech. There is no such thing as hate speech. There is no such thing as hate speech. There is no such thing as hate speech. There is no such thing as hate speech.

There is no such thing as hate speech. There is no such thing as hate speech. There is no such thing as hate speech. There is no such thing as hate speech. There is no such thing as hate speech. There is no such thing as hate speech. There is no such thing as hate speech. There is no such thing as hate speech. There is no such thing as hate speech. There is no such thing as hate speech. There is no such thing as hate speech.

There is no such thing as hate speech. There is no such thing as hate speech. There is no such thing as hate speech. There is no such thing as hate speech. There is no such thing as hate speech. There is no such thing as hate speech. There is no such thing as hate speech.

...there is no such thing as hate speech.

There is no such thing as hate speech. There is no such thing as hate speech. There is no such thing as hate speech.

There is no such thing as hate speech. There is no such thing as hate speech. There is no such thing as hate speech. There is no such thing as hate speech. There is no such thing as hate speech. There is no such thing as hate speech. There is no such thing as hate speech. There is no such thing as hate speech.

There is no such thing as hate speech. There is no such thing as hate speech. There is no such thing as hate speech. There is no such thing as hate speech. There is no such thing as hate speech. There is no such thing as hate speech. There is no such thing as hate speech. There is no such thing as hate speech. There is no such thing as hate speech. There is no such thing as hate speech. There is no such thing as hate speech. There is no such thing as hate speech. There is no such thing as hate speech. There is no such thing as hate speech.

There is no such thing as hate speech. There is no such thing as hate speech.

There is no such thing as hate speech. There is no such thing as hate speech. There is no such thing as hate speech. There is no such thing as hate speech. There is no such thing as hate speech. There is no such thing as hate speech. There is no such thing as hate speech. There is no such thing as hate speech. There is no such thing as hate speech. There is no such thing as hate speech.

There is no such thing as hate speech. There is no such thing as hate speech. There is no such thing as hate speech. There is no such thing as hate speech. There is no such thing as hate speech. There is no such thing as hate speech. There is no such thing as hate speech. There is no such thing as hate speech. There is no such thing as hate speech. There is no such thing as

hate speech. There is no such thing as hate speech. There is no such thing as hate speech. There is no such thing as hate speech. There is no such thing as hate speech. There is no such thing as hate speech. There is no such thing as hate speech. There is no such thing as hate speech. There is no such thing as hate speech. There is no such thing as hate speech.

There is no such thing as hate speech. There is no such thing as hate speech. There is no such thing as hate speech. There is no such thing as hate speech. There is no such thing as hate speech. There is no such thing as hate speech. There is no such thing as hate speech. There is no such thing as hate speech. There is no such thing as hate speech. There is no such thing as hate speech.

There is no such thing as hate speech. There is no such thing as hate speech. There is no such thing as hate speech. There is no such thing as hate speech. There is no such thing as

hate speech. There is no such thing as hate speech. There is no such thing as hate speech. There is no such thing as hate speech. There is no such thing as hate speech. There is no such thing as hate speech. There is no such thing as hate speech. There is no such thing as hate speech. There is no such thing as hate speech. There is no such thing as hate speech. There is no such thing as hate speech. There is no such thing as hate speech. There is no such thing as hate speech. There is no such thing as hate speech. There is no such thing as hate speech. There is no such thing as hate speech. There is no such thing as hate speech. There is no such thing as hate speech. There is no such thing as hate speech.

There is no such thing as hate speech. There is no such thing as hate speech. There is no such thing as hate speech. There is no such thing as hate speech. There is no such thing as hate speech. There is no such thing as hate

speech. There is no such thing as hate speech. There is no such thing as hate speech. There is no such thing as hate speech. There is no such thing as hate speech. There is no such thing as hate speech. There is no such thing as hate speech. There is no such thing as hate speech. There is no such thing as hate speech. There is no such thing as hate speech. There is no such thing as hate speech.

There is no such thing as hate speech. There is no such thing as hate speech. There is no such thing as hate speech. There is no such thing as hate speech. There is no such thing as hate speech. There is no such thing as hate speech. There is no such thing as hate speech. There is no such thing as hate speech. There is no such thing as hate speech. There is no such thing as hate speech. There is no such thing as hate speech.

24

Never Regret Your Words

There is no such thing as hate speech. There is no such thing as hate speech. There is no such thing as hate speech. There is no such thing as hate speech. There is no such thing as hate speech. There is no such thing as hate speech. There is no such thing as hate speech. There is no such thing as hate speech. There is no such thing as hate speech.

There is no such thing as hate speech. There is no such thing as hate speech. There is no such thing as hate speech. There is no such thing as hate speech. There is no such thing as

hate speech. There is no such thing as hate speech. There is no such thing as hate speech. There is no such thing as hate speech. There is no such thing as hate speech.

There is no such thing as hate speech. There is no such thing as hate speech. There is no such thing as hate speech. There is no such thing as hate speech. There is no such thing as hate speech. There is no such thing as hate speech. There is no such thing as hate speech. There is no such thing as hate speech. There is no such thing as hate speech. There is no such thing as hate speech.

There is no such thing as hate speech. There is no such thing as hate speech. There is no such thing as hate speech. There is no such thing as hate speech. There is no such thing as hate speech. There is no such thing as hate speech. There is no such thing as hate speech.

There is no
such thing as
hate speech.

There is no such thing as hate speech. There is no such thing as hate speech. There is no such thing as hate speech. There is no such thing as hate speech. There is no such thing as hate speech. There is no such thing as hate speech. There is no such thing as hate speech. There is no such thing as hate speech. There is no such thing as hate speech. There is no such thing as hate speech. There is no such thing as hate speech.

There is no such thing as hate speech. There is no such thing as hate speech. There is no such thing as hate speech. There is no such thing as hate speech. There is no such thing as hate speech. There is no such thing as hate speech. There is no such thing as hate speech. There is no such thing as hate speech. There is no such thing as hate speech. There is no such thing as hate speech. There is no such thing as hate speech. There is no such thing as hate speech.

There is no such thing as hate speech. There is no such thing as hate speech.

There is no such thing as hate speech. There is no such thing as hate speech. There is no such thing as hate speech. There is no such thing as hate speech. There is no such thing as hate speech. There is no such thing as hate speech. There is no such thing as hate speech. There is no such thing as hate speech. There is no such thing as hate speech. There is no such thing as hate speech. There is no such thing as hate speech.

There is no such thing as hate speech. There is no such thing as hate speech. There is no such thing as hate speech. There is no such thing as hate speech. There is no such thing as hate speech. There is no such thing as hate speech. There is no such thing as hate speech. There is no such thing as hate speech. There is no such thing as hate speech. There is no such thing as hate speech. There is no such thing as

hate speech. There is no such thing as hate speech. There is no such thing as hate speech. There is no such thing as hate speech. There is no such thing as hate speech. There is no such thing as hate speech. There is no such thing as hate speech. There is no such thing as hate speech. There is no such thing as hate speech. There is no such thing as hate speech.

There is no such thing as hate speech. There is no such thing as hate speech. There is no such thing as hate speech. There is no such thing as hate speech. There is no such thing as hate speech. There is no such thing as hate speech. There is no such thing as hate speech. There is no such thing as hate speech. There is no such thing as hate speech. There is no such thing as hate speech.

There is no such thing as hate speech. There is no such thing as hate speech. There is no such thing as hate speech. There is no such thing as hate speech. There is no such thing as

hate speech. There is no such thing as hate speech. There is no such thing as hate speech. There is no such thing as hate speech. There is no such thing as hate speech. There is no such thing as hate speech. There is no such thing as hate speech. There is no such thing as hate speech. There is no such thing as hate speech. There is no such thing as hate speech. There is no such thing as hate speech. There is no such thing as hate speech. There is no such thing as hate speech. There is no such thing as hate speech. There is no such thing as hate speech. There is no such thing as hate speech. There is no such thing as hate speech. There is no such thing as hate speech. There is no such thing as hate speech.

There is no such thing as hate speech. There is no such thing as hate speech. There is no such thing as hate speech. There is no such thing as hate speech. There is no such thing as hate speech. There is no such thing as hate

speech. There is no such thing as hate speech. There is no such thing as hate speech. There is no such thing as hate speech. There is no such thing as hate speech. There is no such thing as hate speech. There is no such thing as hate speech. There is no such thing as hate speech. There is no such thing as hate speech. There is no such thing as hate speech. There is no such thing as hate speech.

There is no such thing as hate speech. There is no such thing as hate speech. There is no such thing as hate speech. There is no such thing as hate speech. There is no such thing as hate speech. There is no such thing as hate speech. There is no such thing as hate speech. There is no such thing as hate speech. There is no such thing as hate speech. There is no such thing as hate speech. There is no such thing as hate speech. There is no such thing as hate speech.

There is no such thing as hate speech. There is no such thing as hate speech. There is no such thing as hate speech. There is no such thing as hate speech. There is no such thing as hate speech. There is no such thing as hate speech. There is no such thing as hate speech. There is no such thing as hate speech. There is no such thing as hate speech. There is no such thing as hate speech. There is no such thing as hate speech. There is no such thing as hate speech. There is no such thing as hate speech. There is no such thing as hate speech. There is no such thing as hate speech. There is no such thing as hate speech.

There is no such thing as hate speech. There is no such thing as hate speech. There is no such thing as hate speech. There is no such thing as hate speech. There is no such thing as hate speech. There is no such thing as hate speech. There is no such thing as hate speech. There is no such thing as hate speech. There is

no such thing as hate speech. There is no such thing as hate speech. There is no such thing as hate speech. There is no such thing as hate speech. There is no such thing as hate speech. There is no such thing as hate speech. There is no such thing as hate speech. There is no such thing as hate speech.

There is no such thing as hate speech. There is no such thing as hate speech. There is no such thing as hate speech. There is no such thing as hate speech. There is no such thing as hate speech. There is no such thing as hate speech. There is no such thing as hate speech. There is no such thing as hate speech. There is no such thing as hate speech. There is no such thing as hate speech. There is no such thing as hate speech.

There is no such thing as hate speech. There is no such thing as hate speech. There is no such thing as hate speech. There is no such

thing as hate speech. There is no such thing as hate speech. There is no such thing as hate speech. There is no such thing as hate speech. There is no such thing as hate speech. There is no such thing as hate speech. There is no such thing as hate speech. There is no such thing as hate speech. There is no such thing as hate speech. There is no such thing as hate speech. There is no such thing as hate speech. There is no such thing as hate speech. There is no such thing as hate speech.

There is no such thing as hate speech. There is no such thing as hate speech. There is no such thing as hate speech. There is no such thing as hate speech. There is no such thing as hate speech. There is no such thing as hate speech. There is no such thing as hate speech. There is no such thing as hate speech. There is no such thing as hate speech. There is no such thing as hate speech. There is no such thing as hate speech. There is no such thing as hate

speech. There is no such thing as hate speech. There is no such thing as hate speech. There is no such thing as hate speech. There is no such thing as hate speech.

There is no such thing as hate speech. There is no such thing as hate speech. There is no such thing as hate speech. There is no such thing as hate speech. There is no such thing as hate speech. There is no such thing as hate speech. There is no such thing as hate speech. There is no such thing as hate speech. There is no such thing as hate speech. There is no such thing as hate speech. There is no such thing as hate speech. There is no such thing as hate speech.

25

Fashionable Speech

There is no such thing as hate speech. There is no such thing as hate speech. There is no such thing as hate speech.

There is no such thing as hate speech. There is no such thing as hate speech. There is no such thing as hate speech. There is no such thing as hate speech. There is no such thing as hate speech. There is no such thing as hate speech.

There is no such thing as hate speech. There is no such thing as hate speech. There is no such thing as hate speech. There is no such

thing as hate speech. There is no such thing as hate speech. There is no such thing as hate speech. There is no such thing as hate speech. There is no such thing as hate speech. There is no such thing as hate speech.

There is no such thing as hate speech. There is no such thing as hate speech. There is no such thing as hate speech. There is no such thing as hate speech. There is no such thing as hate speech. There is no such thing as hate speech. There is no such thing as hate speech. There is no such thing as hate speech. There is no such thing as hate speech. There is no such thing as hate speech.

There is no such thing as hate speech. There is no such thing as hate speech. There is no such thing as hate speech. There is no such thing as hate speech. There is no such thing as hate speech. There is no such thing as hate speech. There is no such thing as hate speech.

There is no such thing as hate speech.

There is no such thing as hate speech. There is no such thing as hate speech. There is no such thing as hate speech.

There is no such thing as hate speech. There is no such thing as hate speech. There is no such thing as hate speech. There is no such thing as hate speech. There is no such thing as hate speech. There is no such thing as hate speech. There is no such thing as hate speech. There is no such thing as hate speech.

"There is no such thing as hate speech. There is no such thing as hate speech. There is no such thing as hate speech. There is no such thing as hate speech."

There is no such thing as hate speech. There is no such thing as hate speech. There is no such thing as hate speech. There is no such thing as hate speech. There is no such thing as hate speech. There is no such thing as hate

speech. There is no such thing as hate speech. There is no such thing as hate speech. There is no such thing as hate speech. There is no such thing as hate speech. There is no such thing as hate speech.

"There is no such thing as hate speech. There is no such thing as hate speech. There is no such thing as hate speech. There is no such thing as hate speech. There is no such thing as hate speech. There is no such thing as hate speech. There is no such thing as hate speech. There is no such thing as hate speech. There is no such thing as hate speech. There is no such thing as hate speech."

There is no such thing as hate speech. There is no such thing as hate speech. There is no such thing as hate speech. There is no such thing as hate speech. There is no such thing as hate

speech. There is no such thing as hate speech. There is no such thing as hate speech. There is no such thing as hate speech. There is no such thing as hate speech.

"There is no such thing as hate speech. There is no such thing as hate speech. There is no such thing as hate speech. There is no such thing as hate speech. There is no such thing as hate speech. There is no such thing as hate speech."

There is no such thing as hate speech. There is no such thing as hate speech. There is no such thing as hate speech. There is no such thing as hate speech.

There is no such thing as hate speech. There is no such thing as hate speech. There is no such thing as hate speech. There is no such thing as hate speech. There is no such thing as hate speech. There is no such thing as hate speech. There is no such thing as hate speech.

There is no such thing as hate speech. There is no such thing as hate speech. There is no such thing as hate speech.

There is no such thing as hate speech. There is no such

thing as hate speech. There is no such thing as hate speech.

There is no such thing as hate speech. There is no such thing as hate speech. There is no such thing as hate speech. There is no such thing as hate speech. There is no such thing as hate speech. There is no such thing as hate speech. There is no such thing as hate speech. There is no such thing as hate speech. There is no such thing as hate speech. There is no such thing as hate speech. There is no such thing as hate speech. There is no such thing as hate speech. There is no such thing as hate speech. There is no such thing as hate speech. There is no such thing as hate speech.

There is no such thing as hate speech. There is no such thing as hate speech. There is no such thing as hate speech. There is no such thing as hate speech. There is no such thing as hate speech. There is no such thing as hate

speech. There is no such thing as hate speech. There is no such thing as hate speech. There is no such thing as hate speech. There is no such thing as hate speech. There is no such thing as hate speech. There is no such thing as hate speech.

26

The Time I Spoke to You

There is no such thing as hate speech. There is no such thing as hate speech. There is no such thing as hate speech. There is no such thing as hate speech. There is no such thing as hate speech. There is no such thing as hate speech. There is no such thing as hate speech. There is no such thing as hate speech. There is no such thing as hate speech.

There is no such thing as hate speech. There is no such thing as hate speech. There is no such thing as hate speech. There is no such thing as hate speech. There is no such thing as

hate speech. There is no such thing as hate speech. There is no such thing as hate speech. There is no such thing as hate speech. There is no such thing as hate speech.

There is no such thing as hate speech. There is no such thing as hate speech. There is no such thing as hate speech. There is no such thing as hate speech. There is no such thing as hate speech. There is no such thing as hate speech. There is no such thing as hate speech. There is no such thing as hate speech. There is no such thing as hate speech. There is no such thing as hate speech. There is no such thing as hate speech.

There is no such thing as hate speech. There is no such thing as hate speech. There is no such thing as hate speech. There is no such thing as hate speech. There is no such thing as hate speech. There is no such thing as hate speech. There is no such thing as hate speech.

There is no
such thing as
hate speech.

There is no such thing as hate speech. There is no such thing as hate speech. There is no such thing as hate speech.

> *"There is…"*
>
> *"…no such thing", as hate speech. There is no such, thing as hate speech!"*
>
> *"There is no such thing as hate speech. There is no such thing. As hate speech. There is no,"*
>
> *"Such thing as hate speech. There is no such thing as hate speech. There is…no such thing as hate speech. There is no such thing as hate speech. There…Is no such thing as hate speech!"*
>
> *"There is no such thing", as hate speech. There is no such, thing as hate speech?"*

There is no such thing as hate speech. There is no such thing as hate speech. There is no such thing as hate speech. There is no such thing as

hate speech. There is no such thing as hate speech. There is no such thing as hate speech. There is no such thing as hate speech. There is no such thing as hate speech.

There is no such thing as hate speech. There is no such thing as hate speech. There is no such thing as hate speech. There is no such thing as hate speech. There is no such thing as hate speech. There is no such thing as hate speech. There is no such thing as hate speech. There is no such thing as hate speech. There is no such thing as hate speech. There is no such thing as hate speech. There is no such thing as hate speech. There is no such thing as hate speech. There is no such thing as hate speech. There is no such thing as hate speech.

"There is no such thing", as hate speech. There is no such, thing as hate speech!"

"There is no such thing as hate speech. There is no such thing."

"As hate speech. There is no,"

"Such thing as hate speech. There is no such thing as hate speech. There is,"

"No such thing as hate speech. There is no such thing as hate speech. There…Is no such thing as hate speech!"

"There is no such thing", as hate speech. There is no such, thing as hate speech?"

"There is no such thing", as hate speech. There is no such, thing as hate speech."

"There is no such thing as hate speech. There is no such thing."

"As hate speech. There is no,"

"Such thing as hate speech. There is no such thing as hate speech. There is,"

"…no such thing as hate speech. There is no such thing as hate speech. There…Is no such thing as hate speech!"

"There is no such thing", as hate speech. There is no such, thing as hate speech?"
"There is…"
"No such thing", as hate speech. There is no such, thing as hate speech?"
"There is no such thing as hate speech. There is no such thing."
"As hate speech. There is no. Such thing as hate speech. There is no such thing as hate speech. There is,"
"No such thing as hate speech. There is no such thing as hate speech. There…Is no such thing as hate speech! There is no such thing", as hate speech. There is no such, thing as hate speech?"
"There is no such thing", as hate speech. There is no such, thing as hate speech!"
"There is no such thing as hate speech. There is no such thing."
"As hate speech. There is no,"

> *"Such thing as hate speech. There is no such thing as hate speech. There is,"*
> *"…no such thing as hate speech. There is no such thing as hate speech. There…Is no such thing as hate speech!"*
> *"There is no such thing", as hate speech. There is no such, thing as hate speech?"*

There is no such thing as hate speech. There is no such thing as hate speech. There is no such thing as hate speech. There is no such thing as hate speech. There is no such thing as hate speech. There is no such thing as hate speech. There is no such thing as hate speech. There is no such thing as hate speech. There is no such thing as hate speech. There is no such thing as hate speech. There is no such thing as hate speech.

There is no such thing as hate speech. There is no such thing as hate speech. There is no such thing as hate speech. There is no such

thing as hate speech. There is no such thing as hate speech. There is no such thing as hate speech. There is no such thing as hate speech. There is no such thing as hate speech. There is no such thing as hate speech. There is no such thing as hate speech. There is no such thing as hate speech. There is no such thing as hate speech. There is no such thing as hate speech. There is no such thing as hate speech. There is no such thing as hate speech. There is no such thing as hate speech. There is no such thing as hate speech. There is no such thing as hate speech. There is no such thing as hate speech. There is no such thing as hate speech.

There is no such thing as hate speech. There is no such thing as hate speech. There is no such thing as hate speech. There is no such thing as hate speech. There is no such thing as hate speech. There is no such thing as hate speech. There is no such thing as hate speech. There is no such thing as hate speech. There is

no such thing as hate speech. There is no such thing as hate speech.

There is no such thing as hate speech. There is no such thing as hate speech. There is no such thing as hate speech. There is no such thing as hate speech. There is no such thing as hate speech. There is no such thing as hate speech. There is no such thing as hate speech. There is no such thing as hate speech. There is no such thing as hate speech. There is no such thing as hate speech. There is no such thing as hate speech.

> *"There is no such thing as hate speech. There is no such, thing as hate speech!"*
> *"There is no such thing as hate speech. There is no such thing."*
> *"As hate speech. There is no,"*
> *"Such thing as hate speech. There is no such thing as hate speech. There is no such thing as hate speech. There is no such thing as hate*

speech. There…Is no such thing as hate speech!"
"There is no such thing", as hate speech. There is no such, thing as hate speech?"

There is no such thing as hate speech. There is no such thing as hate speech. There is no such thing as hate speech. There is no such thing as hate speech. There is no such thing as hate speech. There is no such thing as hate speech. There is no such thing as hate speech. There is no such thing as hate speech. There is no such thing as hate speech. There is no such thing as hate speech. There is no such thing as hate speech. There is no such thing as hate speech.

There is no such thing as hate speech. There is no such thing as hate speech. There is no such thing as hate speech. There is no such thing as hate speech. There is no such thing as hate speech. There is no such thing as hate

speech. There is no such thing as hate speech. There is no such thing as hate speech. There is no such thing as hate speech. There is no such thing as hate speech. There is no such thing as hate speech. There is no such thing as hate speech. There is no such thing as hate speech. There is no such thing as hate speech. There is no such thing as hate speech. There is no such thing as hate speech. There is no such thing as hate speech.

There is no such thing as hate speech. There is no such thing as hate speech. There is no such thing as hate speech. There is no such thing as hate speech. There is no such thing as hate speech. There is no such thing as hate speech. There is no such thing as hate speech. There is no such thing as hate speech. There is no such thing as hate speech. There is no such thing as hate speech. There is no such thing as hate speech. There is no such thing as hate speech.

Conclusion

References

Constitution of United States of America 1789 | Amendment 1 | Congress shall make no law respecting an establishment of religion, or prohibiting the free exercise thereof; or abridging the freedom of speech, or of the press; or the right of the people peaceably to assemble, and to petition the Government for a redress of grievances.

National Gallery of Art

Title: Self-Portrait | Artist: Judith Leyster | Dated: c. 1630 | Page 5

Title: George Washington | Artist: Gilbert Stuart | Dated: 1795 | Page: xiii

Title: The Lute Player and the Singer | Artist: Israhel van Meckenem | Dated: c. 1495/1503 | Page xviii

Title: A Girl with a Flower in Her Hair | Artist: Pietro Rotari | Dated: 1760/1762 | Page 3/Cover

Title: Saint Cecilia and an Angel | Artist: Orazio Gentileschi and Giovanni Lanfranco | Dated: c. 1617/1618 and c. 1621/1627 | Page 11

Title: Self-Portrait | Artist: Paul Gauguin | Dated: 1889 | Page 21

Title: Alexander Condemning False Praise | Artist: Francesco de Mura | Dated: 1760s | Page 31

Title: The Artist's Brother-in-Law, Ludwig Hassenpflug, Preparing to Play the Piano | Artist: Ludwig Emil Grimm | Dated: 1826 | Page 39

Title: The Loge | Artist: Mary Cassatt | Dated: 1882 | Page 47

Title: The Artist's Father, Reading "L'Événement" | Artist: Paul Cézanne | Dated: 1866 | Page 55

Title: The Trinity | Artist: Domenico Piola I | Dated: 1627 – 1703 | Page 65

Title: Girl with a Flute | Artist: Attributed to Johannes Vermeer | Dated: probably 1665/1670 | Page 73

Title: Girl in White | Artist: Vincent van Gogh | Dated: 1890 | Page 85

Made in the USA
Monee, IL
25 March 2021